Introducing Lan[...]

Getting to know L[...]   6
Settling in   [1]0
Getting around   [1]2
The language   14

Don't miss

The best of Lanzarote   16
The best of Fuerteventura   18

Lanzarote Resorts

Arrecife   20   Matagorda   40
Puerto del Carmen   28   Playa Blanca   44
Playa de los Pocillos   36   Costa Teguise   50

Lanzarote Excursions

Timanfaya National Park   56   Central Lanzarote   70
Northern Lanzarote   64   Southern Lanzarote 76

Fuerteventura Resorts

Caleta de Fustes (El Castillo)   80
Playa Jandía   86
Costa Calma   88
Corralejo   92

Fuerteventura Excursions

Northern Fuerteventura   98
Southern Fuerteventura   102

Lifestyles

Food and drink   108
Menu decoder   110
Shopping   112
Kids   114
Sports and activities   116
Festivals and events   118
Taking better holiday photos   120

Practical information

Getting to Lanzarote and Fuerteventura   124
First-time traveller's guide   125

Written and researched by
Brian and Eileen Anderson: updated by Jill Benjamin

The contents of this guidebook are believed correct at the time of printing. Attractions and establishments may open, close or change and Thomas Cook Holdings Ltd cannot accept responsibility for errors or omissions, or for the consequences of any reliance on the information provided. Descriptions and assessments are based on the author's views and experience at the time of writing and these do not necessarily represent those of Thomas Cook Holdings. We would be grateful to be told of any changes or updates; please notify them to the Commissioning Editor at the address below.

Thomas Cook Publishing, Thomas Cook Holdings Ltd, PO Box 227, Peterborough PE3 8XX, United Kingdom.
E-mail: books@thomascook.com

Opposite: The Jardín de Cactus on Lanzarote

LA PALMA

■ Santa Cruz de la Palma

TENERIFE

Puerto de la Cruz ■

■ Santa Cruz de Tenerife

GOMERA

■ San Sebastián de la Gomera

■ Los Cristianos

HIERRO

■ Valverde

ATLANTIC OCEAN

ATLANTIC OCEAN

Airport

Costa Teguise

LANZAROTE

Arrecife

Puerto del Carmen

Playa Blanca

Corralejo

FUERTEVENTURA

Puerto del Rosario

Airport

Caleta de Fuste

Gran Tarajal

GRAN CANARIA

Morro Jable

Jandía Playa

Las Palmas

Puerto de Mogán

0   50 km

Getting to know Lanzarote and Fuerteventura

Lanzarote and Fuerteventura are two of the most popular islands in the Canaries and with good reason. They seem to have enough sand between them to restock the Sahara! Finding space to pitch a sunbed or towel to soak in the hot rays of a relentless sun will not be a problem. The major decision of the day may simply be to decide which beach to lie on.

Lanzarote's inviting seas

Life beyond the beach stretches into the crashing, foaming white waves which lap these shores. Sheltered beaches and coves abound, but for surfing and windsurfing enthusiasts looking to test their skills, there are miles of opportunities – great fun not just for the participants but also for those spectating prone from a sunbed. Other watery activities are available, too, in the form of scuba diving, deep-sea fishing or cruising for the sheer pleasure of being out on the coastal waters.

Intriguing volcanic landscapes await those venturing inland. Different from anything found elsewhere in Europe, colour-washed barren hills, black fields and solitary palms present haunting, unforgettable images. The ultimate experience of volcanic landscapes is provided by the Timanfaya National Park (*see page 56*), easily accessible from both islands.

ISLAND CHARACTER

Fuerteventura is the quieter of the two islands, good for a laid-back holiday, with delightfully empty roads when the time comes to explore. Betancuria, the old capital, is the cultural highspot, but there are other equally fascinating visits to make.

On Lanzarote, the name of César Manrique will crop up again and again – his contribution to the island's art and culture is inescapable (*see below*). Influenced by the island's unique landscape, César Manrique turned to designing attractions that harmonise with nature and inject energy and colour.

ABOUT THE ISLANDS

Volcanic activity, some 3 million years ago, produced a group of islands off the coast of Africa now known as the Canary Islands. Fuerteventura and Lanzarote are the two most easterly islands of the group.

Fuerteventura is the second largest island in the Canaries after Tenerife and appreciably larger than Lanzarote. Its sandy beaches number more than 100 and its highest mountain, Pico de la Zarza near Jandía, reaches to an altitude of 2,647ft (807m). All the major resorts on the island are found on the sheltered eastern or southern coasts.

Lanzarote enjoys more modest proportions. It measures only 39.75 miles (62km) north to south and 13.1 miles (21km) east to west, and it rises to 671m (2,201ft).

CÉSAR MANRIQUE

Born in Arrecife on 24 April 1919, César Manrique left the island to pursue his love of art in Madrid and New York, building an international reputation. He returned to Lanzarote in 1968 and devoted his immense talent and energy to the benefit of the island, creating such major tourist attractions as the Jardín del Cactus (*page 69*) and the Castillo de San José (*page 24*). He died in a car accident on 25 September 1992, at the age of 73, but his artistry has left an indelible mark on the island and will influence the thinking of generations to come.

Opposite: Straw weaving on Fuerteventura

Settling in

MONEY MATTERS

Currency: In line with the majority of EU member states, Spain entered the single currency on 1 Jan 2002, with the peseta accepted as dual currency up to 28 February. Euro (€) note denominations are 500, 200, 100, 50, 20, 10 and 5. Coins are 1 and 2 euros and 1, 2, 5, 10, 20 and 50 céntimos. A euro equals 166.386 pesetas.

Banks: open 0830–1415 from Monday to Friday; some open 0900–1300 on Saturday. Most banks offer cash machine facilities for UK bank and credit cards including Eurocheque cards. Exchange bureaux are indicated by a Cambio sign.

 The highest exchange rate is only a good deal if the commission charged is not excessive.

SHOPS AND SERVICES

Shops: general shopping hours are 0900–1300 and 1700–2000. Sunday is a general closing day. Shopping hours are not rigidly followed, especially in tourist areas. Supermarkets and bread shops are often open earlier, usually at 0830, and there are always some which stay open all day. Many shops relying on tourist trade stay open until late evening, closing around 2200.

Telephones: clear multilingual instructions are displayed in direct-dial booths. Phonecards can be purchased from local shops and will save you having to carry pockets full of change to the public call box.

 The cheapest time to call home is after 2000 Saturday and all day Sunday.

DIALLING ABROAD
The dialling code for international access is **00**. Wait until a second dialling tone is heard, then dial the country code (UK = **44**), followed by the area code (without the initial zero) and the subscriber number.

BEACH SAFETY

A flag system is used to warn bathers when sea conditions are unsafe for swimming.

- Red flag: dangerous conditions, no swimming.
- Yellow: good swimmers only, apply caution.
- Green: safe bathing conditions.

HEALTH AND HYGIENE

Sunbathing: the sun is very strong at all times of the year so take great care with sunbathing. Cooling breezes often disguise the heat of the sun. Use high-factor creams initially and limit your sunbathing hours. Cover up at midday and in the early afternoon when the sun is at its highest. Remember, a slow tan is deeper and lasts longer. Do not let sunburn ruin your holiday.

 TIP! Tap water is produced by desalination. It is not unsafe but does not taste good and is rich in minerals which can cause upset stomachs. It is recommended that you drink bottled water.

CRIME AND EMERGENCIES

Crime prevention: take as much care of your personal property as you would at home. Watch out for pickpockets, especially in crowded market places. Crime with violence is unusual, but don't take risks. Leave nothing of value in a parked car, not even locked in the boot. Bag snatchers are around, too, so carry your valuables in a bag securely anchored to your body.

Lost property: report any loss or theft to your holiday representative. If an insurance claim is to be made, you must report thefts within 24 hours to the Municipal Police or Guardia Civil, from whom an official report must be obtained.

Police: if you have a problem – say with lost or stolen property – talk to your holiday rep or hotel desk; they can help you make an official statement to the police.

WHAT TO DO IN AN EMERGENCY

Fuerteventura and Lanzarote: Emergency services, **tel: 112**

Getting around

Buses: current bus timetables are available from tourist offices. A regular and reliable bus service operates on both islands. Like the spokes of a wheel, buses mostly operate directly into and out of the capital. This means a change of bus is often necessary to reach a particular destination. It pays to be on the early side since buses sometimes run marginally ahead of schedule. Not all services operate on Sunday. The Canarian word for bus, *guagua*, is pronounced '*wah-wah*'.

Lanzarote: The main resorts are connected to the capital, Arrecife, with a frequent bus service, mostly half hourly.

Fuerteventura: coastal services run out from the capital, Puerto del Rosario, to Caleta de Fustes and Corralejo at half hourly intervals for most of the day. Jandía (Morro Jable) is well served, too, but only a very limited service operates to other destinations.

Taxis: Official taxis are easily recognised by the sign on the roof. Next to the sign is a light which shows green when the taxi is free. Generally, short journeys within town are not expensive, especially with four people sharing. The taxis are colour-coded according to the district in which they operate. For longer journeys outside town, agree a price beforehand.

Car hire: There are plenty of opportunities for hiring a car on the island. Your holiday representative can help with this.

RULES OF THE ROAD

Remember to drive on the right! Motorists must carry their driving licence, passport and car hire documents at all times. Failure to do so will result in an automatic on-the-spot fine if you are stopped in one of the frequent road checks.

In general, the road surfaces are good. Road markings are clear but some of the traffic systems can be confusing when first encountered. Be aware that traffic priorities in these complex traffic systems do not always conform to your expectations: you might find a stop sign part way round a roundabout

SPEED LIMITS

- Neither Lanzarote nor Fuerteventura have motorways.
- Autovia (primary road) 100 kph.
- Carretera (A road) 80 kph.
- Built-up areas 40 kph.

or even on a main highway.

Petrol is cheap on the islands and petrol stations are frequent along main routes. Always fill up with petrol before heading off into the hills or the interior.

Parking meters are usual in built-up or popular areas. Here the parking spaces are marked out in blue. Pay at the meter and display the ticket on the windscreen. Parking in side streets is generally allowed except where the kerbstones are painted yellow (or green and white in bus-stop areas). Illegal parking results in the car being towed away.

A few useful words for drivers:

- *Aparcamiento* means parking.
- *Estacionamiento Prohibido* means no parking.
- *Ceda al Paso* means give way to the right and left.
- *Circunvalación* means ring road.

 Most road maps are fairly accurate, but they have not caught up with the new road numbering system, whose numbers bear no relationship to the old. The original GC road numbers have been abolished and FZ road numbers are used instead on Fuerteventura, and LZ numbers on Lanzarote.

ORGANISED TOURS

For those not keen to drive on holiday or just happy to sit back and let others take the strain, there are plenty of organised tours to all parts of the island. Some of the inland locations are poorly served by public transport and an organised excursion offers the best option.

 Beware of illegal operators offering very cheap tours. Either they may be operating without insurance or they may take your money and disappear.

The language

The Canarians respond warmly to visitors who attempt to speak a little of their language. Here are a few words and phrases to get you going:

HOTEL

hotel	*el hotel*
room	*la habitación*
single/double	*individual/doble*
one/two nights	*una/dos noches*
per person/per room	*por persona/por habitación*
reservation	*la reserva*
rate	*el precio*
breakfast	*el desayuno*
toilet	*los servicious/aseos*
bath	*el baño*
shower	*la ducha*
en suite	*en su habitación*
balcony	*el balcón*
key	*la llave*
chambermaid	*la camarera*

MONEY

bank	*el banco*
exchange bureau	*la oficina de cambio*
post office	*correos*
cashier	*el cajero*
money	*el dinero*
coin	*la moneda*
foreign currency	*la moneda extranjera*
change money	*cambiar dinero*
bank card	*la tarjeta del banco*
credit card	*la tarjeta del crédito*
cheque	*el talon, cheque*
traveller's cheque	*el cheque de viaje*

EATING OUT

restaurant	*el restaurante*
bar	*el bar*
table	*la mesa*
menu	*la carta*
tourist menu	*el menú turístico*
set menu	*el menú del dia*
wine list	*la carta de vinos*
lunch	*el almuerzo*

dinner	*la cena*
snack	*tapa/s*
starter	*el primer plato*
dish	*el plato*
main course	*el plato principal*
dessert	*el postre*
drink	*la bebida*
waiter	*el camarero*
bill	*la cuenta*

TRAVEL

aeroplane	*el avion*
airport	*el aeropuerto*
flight	*el vuelo*
bus	*guagua*
station	*la estación de guagua*
stop	*la parada de guagua*
ferry	*el ferry*
port	*el puerto*
ticket	*el billete*
single/return	*ida/ida y vuelta*
timetable	*el horario*
seat	*el asiento*
free	*libre*
reserved	*reservado*
non-smoking	*no fumadores*

GENERAL VOCABULARY

yes	*sí*
no	*no*
please	*por favor*
thank you	*(muchas) gracias*
hello	*hola*
goodbye	*adiós*
good day	*buenos días*
good afternoon	*buenas tardes*
good night	*buenas noches*
excuse me	*perdón*
help!	*¡socorro!*
today	*hoy*
tomorrow	*mañana*
yesterday	*ayer*
how much?	*¿cuánto?*
expensive	*caro*
open	*abierto*
closed	*cerrado*

Lanzarote landscape with flowers

The best of Lanzarote

BEACHES

Gorgeous beaches of pure golden Sahara sand – not the grainy black stuff more typical of the other Canaries – await you here in the south of Lanzarote. The sun-baked beaches of Puerto del Carmen (*page 28*) make it the largest and busiest resort, adjoined by its quieter sister beaches of Playa de los Pocillos (*page 36*) and Matagorda (*page 40*). The most northerly of the resorts, Costa Teguise (*page 50*) has five glorious sandy beaches and benefits from a welcome, cooling breeze. On the southern tip, Playa Blanca (*page 44*) has perhaps the prettiest beaches of all and sun-worshippers flock to the famous Papagayo (parrot) Beaches (*page 47*), probably the finest on the whole island.

AWAY FROM THE COAST

The whole island of Lanzarote has been designated a Biosphere Reserve by Unesco (United Nations Organisation for Education, Science and Culture); this designation is aimed at maintaining its cultural heritage and protecting the quality of life. Lanzarote has avoided over-development and the contribution that the late César Manrique played in turning the island's natural assets into top attractions is unmatched anywhere in the world. His life's mission was to create a symbol of quality around the stunning natural beauty of his island, so far from being just volcanic and barren. His works include:

- **Fundación César Manrique** (*page 72*): his own incredible house built in the middle of a petrified stream of lava, where the original landowner refused to take money for what he considered to be a heap of volcanic slag!

- **Jameos del Agua** (*page 68*): an exotic subterranean garden in an underground volcanic tunnel with an underground lake.

- **Restaurant La Era** (*page 75*): renovated by Cesar Manrique.

- **Jardín de Cactus** (*page 69*): extraordinary garden of over 1,400 varieties of cactus from shapes like wedding cakes covered in hair to porcupines and prickly rockets, all set in a former disused quarry, transformed by Manrique.

THE BEST OF THE REST

Timanfaya National Park

Created to protect an area of volcanic activity which devastated the island in the 18th century, Timanfaya is also called Fire Mountain – with good reason – and features César Manrique's El Diablo restaurant, named after the devil (*page 56*).

Cueva de los Verdes

Enjoy a walk through part of one of the longest lava cave systems in the world (*page 68*).

Betancuria's Cathedral

The best of Fuerteventura

BEACHES

Fuerteventura is the oldest of all the Canary Islands lying just over 60 miles (96km) off the coast of Africa. It is also the second largest, but most sparsely populated of them all. Under African skies, you'll find miles of beautiful, often deserted white sandy beaches, tempered by cooling Atlantic breezes. The inshore waters are perfect for windsurfing and attract some of the world's top windsurfers, culminating in the World Windsurfing Championships held every July/August in Sotavento on the south-eastern shore. Here on the Jandía peninsula, there are 20 miles (32km) of spectacular pale sands, overlooked by the island's tallest peak, the 2,650ft (807m) Pico de Zarza, an extint volcano (also known as *Orejas de Asno* – 'Donkey Ears' – you'll know why as soon as you see it!).

The most impressive single area of dazzling white sand dunes is just beside Corralejo, the island's main resort on the northern tip, where you can easily believe yourself to be in the Sahara. Designated a protected zone (known as the Parque Natural de las Dunas de Corralejo), it also enjoys probably the best sun record of any of the Canary Islands.

AWAY FROM THE COAST

An organised island tour will take in the best beaches and show you some of the scenery of the interior. Or rent a car for a few days and explore the heart of the deserted island scenery, striking volcanic landscape and new but quiet, if you really want to get away from it all. You might even see the white-pawed local dogs, descendants of the wild dogs of Fuerteventura which gave their name to The Canaries (*canis* is Latin for 'dog') – not canary birds as you might imagine!

THE BEST OF THE REST

- A visit to Betancuria (*see page 100*), which served as the island's capital until the mid 19th century. This is a small bright white village oozing with character and charm – fantastic for photo opportunities!

- Take a ride on a camel in south of the island at La Latija (*see page 103*) which also has an excellent zoo. Watch the crocodiles feeding (from a distance!) as well as monkeys, baboons and all kinds of exotic birds including performing parrots that give special daily shows.

- Experience a real desert island, just a short boat trip away from Corralejo, on the Isla de Lobos (*see page 96*). From the lighthouse you get fantastic views of the island and Fuerteventura and, in the other direction, the pale beaches on Lanzarote's southern shore.

Fuerteventura and Lanzarote are only 35 minutes apart by ferry and it is very easy to slip over from one to the other to enjoy a change of scene.

Arrecife's lagoon

Arrecife – Lanzarote's bustling capital

A visit to Arrecife is a must for shopaholics but it also offers a touch of history and an expanse of golden sandy beach. An unexpected bonus is a very pleasant lagoon area, in the heart of town, which provides a welcome oasis for a coffee or lunch break. Everything you will want to see is centrally located and easy to explore.

Arrecife lies on the southern coast of the island, facing Africa, and gets its name from the reefs and tiny islands dotted around the bay. It has been the capital since the 19th century and has two fine fortresses to watch over its harbours. The main beach, La Playa del Reducto, has European Blue Flag status and a palm-lined promenade bustles with cafés, restaurants and souvenir shops. A prominent landmark is the charred ruin of the old Gran Hotel on the waterfront (eastern corner of Playa del Reducto). This is all that remains of the island's first and only multi-storey building.

León y Castillo, the main shopping street, is closed to traffic during shopping hours. There are no big-name stores here but a wide choice of smaller outlets selling just about everything. You can visit the Castillo de San Gabriel (*see below*), locate the Tourist Information centre on the promenade (good for maps and information), stroll to Playa del Reducto beach, then back past more cafés and shops to the lagoon.

TIP! The tourist office in Arrecife is located at 6 Avenida Generalisimo Franco. *Tel: 928 801 517. Open Mon–Fri 0800–1400.*

THINGS TO SEE AND DO

Castillo de San Gabriel *

Connected to the shore by a bridge, this squat round tower (built in 1590) now houses the archaeological museum. On view are artefacts, skulls and a skeleton from the time of the island's earlier inhabitants, the Guanches (also known as Aborigens). There is also an observatory on the roof. *Opposite Avenida Generalisimo Franco. Tel: 928 802 884. Open Tues–Sat 0900–1300 & 1700–1900 in summer. Admission charge. Free entry to observatory on Thur, Fri & Sat 2230–0130.*

TEGUISE

Circunvalación

SAN BARTOLOMÉ

General García Escamez

Vía Medular

General García Escamez

Circunvalación

Doctor Góm

Vía Medular

Bolivia Zaragoza

Triana

Garajonay

Taxi Rank

José Antonio

Avenida Fred Olsen

18 de Julio

La Porra

Coronel Bens

José Betancort

Generalísimo

AIRPORT

PLAYA
DEL REDUCTO

Ca
San

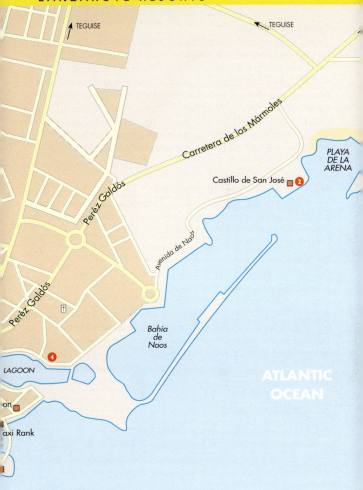

TEGUISE

TEGUISE

Carretera de los Mármoles

PLAYA DE LA ARENA

Castillo de San José ■ ❷

Peréz Galdós

Peréz Galdós

Avenida de Naos

Peréz Galdós

❹

Bahía de Naos

LAGOON

on

ATLANTIC OCEAN

axi Rank

Castillo de San José ★★★

Located on the north side of Arrecife (a short taxi ride along the coast towards the port), this fortress was built as a part of a job-creation scheme in 1776–99. At the time, local people were suffering near-starvation following the major volcanic eruptions that destroyed so much of the island's best agricultural land. The 'castle' is now a museum of modern art, including examples of the work of César Manrique (*see page 8*). It is also a very fine place to enjoy a morning coffee, lunch or an evening meal, admiring the view of the harbour from the bar restaurant. *Carretera de Puerto Naos. Tel: 928 812 321. Gallery open daily 1100–2100. Admission free. Restaurant (£££) open 1300–1545 & 2000–2330. Café/bar (£) open 1100–0100.*

El Charco de San Gines (the Lagoon) ★★

This delightful stretch of inland water is only accessible to small boats. Stroll around the pedestrianised perimeter of the lagoon and choose one of the waterside café/bars or restaurants for lunch or a snack.

BEACHES

Playa del Reducto is a large beach of fine sand, ideal for a sunbathing session and a picnic.

 Buy electrical goods and watches from Visanta or Sam (also good prices on duty-free drink), along the promenade in the town centre. Bargaining may not be an option, but you will get genuine goods, value for money and full international guarantees. If you come here by bus, check out the duty-free prices in the supermarket near the bus station.

EXCURSION

Casa Museo y Monumento al Campesino ★★★

This monument standing at the geographical centre of the island, near San Bartolomé, was built as a tribute to the Lanzarotean farmer, both past and present, by César Manrique. Farming on Lanzarote has always required inventiveness and hard work, but the La Geria wine area shows how successful

SHOPPING

All the following are on the main shopping street, León y Castillo:

Spinola Shopping Centre At first sight, the brown-windowed exterior of the Spinola Shopping Centre resembles a railway station. Inside are four floors of supermarket-style shopping with food on the ground floor and an array of other goods on the floors above. Shops here vie with each other to tempt you to buy duty-free goods (*but see page 113*). There are plenty of boutiques full of the latest fashions and bargains in leather shoes, handbags and belts. Jewellery figures highly, as do perfumes, and there are some unusual craft items which are worth taking home as souvenirs.

El Mercadillo Not to be missed, El Mercadillo is a small shopping centre. Its rustic appeal, with a wooden gallery, glass roof, interesting shops and ambient central café area make it a place to linger.

Behind the post office is a pedestrian square with peaceful snack bars away from the traffic.

Arrecife's Castillo de San Gabriel

they have been. The building and the adjoining *Monument to Fertility* sculpture show traditional Lanzarotean architecture, including 11 arts and crafts workshops set around a large central patio where you can watch artisans making ceramics, embroidery and other traditional local wares using methods handed down from previous generations. There is also a small wine cellar for tasting (and buying!) local wines. Keep sunglasses handy – it is all presented in gleaming white, the green woodwork providing the only relief. The original restaurant (£) serves traditional Lanzarotean-Canarian dishes and is very popular with the locals (open 1230–1630). A 450-seat restaurant (££) is open serving international and local cuisine and has a stage for live performances (1300–1430). *Between San Bartolomé and Mozaga. Tel: 928 520 136. Museum and monument open daily 1000–1700. Admission free.*

RESTAURANTS AND BARS *(see map on pages 22–23)*

 Restaurante Chino Taiwan ££ ❶ Excellent food and service. Busy. Take-away. *Tel: 928 814 562. Open every day.*

 Castillo de San José £££ ❷ For a special treat, lunch or dine at this superb restaurant beneath the castle enjoying panoramic views over the harbour. Excellent local and international dishes. No shorts, sleeveless shirts or T-shirts. *Carretera de Puerto Naos. Tel: 928 812 321. Open daily 1300–1545 & 2000–2330. Booking advised.*

Pizzaria Italiana Gigi £ ❸ Real pizzas. Small and very popular. Take-away. *Averida near Club Nautico (Sailing Club). Tel: 928 814 749. Open Thurs–Tues.*

La Recova £ ❹ Light meals and snacks. Good atmosphere. *Calle Gines de Castro. Tel: 928 807 488. Closed Sat pm and all day Sunday.*

Opposite: The Casa Museo y Monumento al Campesino

Puerto del Carmen –
the island's liveliest resort

Puerto del Carmen has developed from a small fishing village into the largest and liveliest resort on the island. The whole complex stretches eastwards for around 4.5 miles (7km) from the port. The resort incorporates the original village, and the Avenida de las Playas connects Puerto del Carmen to Playa de los Pocillos, and to developing Matagorda, the nearest resort to the airport.

The Avenida de las Playas near Fariones is a wide and pleasant pedestrian walkway – probably the finest in Lanzarote. The promenade is adorned with rustling palm trees, magenta bougainvillaea, wild pink geraniums and hibiscus – and is definitely the place to be seen. Although Puerto del Carmen is almost entirely a new town, there are no high-rise buildings and, despite the huge changes that the town has undergone, it hasn't lost the charm of the original fishing village.

The Avenida de las Playas ribbons along the coast, and visitors can easily connect with the various beaches by bus or taxi. A visit to the port and old centre helps set the scene and adds atmosphere for first-time visitors. From the port, stroll round the coast past the rocky shore – where sub-aqua diving lessons take place – and the small sandy beach of Playa Pequeña. A diversion around Hotel Los Fariones leads to Playa Grande beach. Confusingly, Playa Grande is also known as Playa Blanca, but is not the same as the Playa Blanca in the south (*page 44*). This is the hub of activity in these parts and possibly as far as many will want to go, but shops line the road as far as Los Pocillos.

 There are two tourist kiosks in Puerto del Carmen. They are both on the sea-front. The one by Playa Blanca, near the Red Cross, is open Mon–Fri 1000–1700, Sat 0900–1300; the other, opposite Hard Rock, is open Mon–Fri 0900–1300 & 1700–1900 (1630–1930 in summer), Sat 0900–1300.

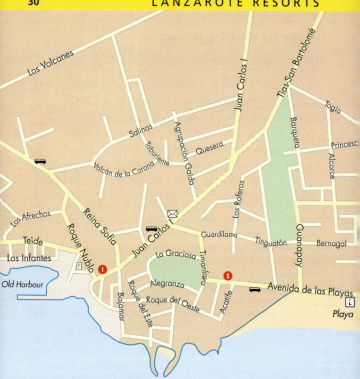

Los Volcanes

Juan Carlos I

Tías-San Bartolomé

Togío

Princesc

Salinas

Agrupación Gaida

Quesera

Barqueta

Alcorce

Taburiente

Volcán de la Corona

Los Roferos

Los Afrechos

Reina Sofía

Juan Carlos

Guardilama

Tinguatón

Guanapay

Bernagal

Teide

Roque Nublo

Los Infantes

La Graciosa

Timanfaya

Old Harbour

Alegranza

Bajamar

Roque del Este

Roque del Oeste

Acatife

Avenida de las Playas

Playa

ATLANTIC

0   250   500 m

Achagua

guise

Princesa Ico

Princesa
Guayarmina

César Manrique

Anzuelo

Timple

Tanausu

Folias

s.

2

Nicaragua

Anzuelo

Palangre

Pedro

Barba

Rociega

Timón

Ancla

Arpón

Chalana

Finlandia

Mirafondo

Suecia

Francia

Avenida de Italia

Frankfurt

MATAGORDA

ARRE

Avenida de las Playas

ande

3

4

OCEAN

Lazy days at Puerto del Carmen

THINGS TO SEE AND DO

Horse riding *
Try the Rancho Texas riding stables, in Puerto del Carmen (*tel: 928 173 247*) or Lanzarote á Caballo, at Yaiza (*tel: 928 830 314*).

Tennis **
Sports Centre Insular, near Fariones Hotel.

Old harbour ***
Just south of Playa Grande (sometimes referred to as Playa Blanca – but not to be confused with Playa Blanca in the south!) lies the small fishing harbour, the heart of the original Puerto del Carmen village. This is a wonderful place

to sit out on the terraces with a long, cool drink, watching the fishing boats and yachts bobbing up and down. In the square next to the port, you can see the locals playing boules and feast on excellent fresh fish served at the harbourside restaurants. For a taste of home, drop in at the buzzing Irish Harbour Bar (£) or Victoria Inn (£), both at Calle Tiede on the harbour. For *tapas* and fresh fish from the fishermen try any of the excellent restaurants on the quay.

Watersports **

There are many opportunities for glass-bottomed boat trips, snorkelling and scuba diving, submarine trips, even deep-sea fishing.

- *Princesa Ico Catamaran* with panoramic underwater windows. Mini cruises to Fuerteventura. *Princess Yaiza* glass-bottomed boat. Trips to Papagayo. Deep sea fishing (marlin or even shark!) *All at the old port of Puerto del Carmen. Tel: 928 512 898.*

- For submarine trips from Puerto Calero *Tel: 928 512 898. Website: www.submarinesafaris.com*

- Island Watersports offers snorkelling and scuba-diving tours and instruction. Fun for al the family. *Calle Bajamar 17 (near old port). Tel: 928 512 563.*

- There are also many fun activities to choose from on the beaches.

EXCURSIONS

There are a number of quite exciting trips to make on the island and many of the locations were designed by César Manrique (*see page 8*). Some of these sights feature in organised excursions, while others can only be visited by car – ask your holiday representative for further details.

BEACHES

Puerto del Carmen's safe and sandy beaches fly the coveted Blue Flag of the EU for cleanliness and hygiene. Playa Grande (Blanca) has sunbeds and umbrellas available for a small charge and plenty of space to pitch your towel, as well as a good choice of cafés and bars on hand.

RESTAURANTS AND BARS *(see map on pages 30–31)*

 The Tartan Teddy £ ❶ Busy, atmospheric. Live music. *At crossroads in old town of Puerto del Carmen. Tel: 928 515 613. Open daily 1000–2000.*

L'artista ££ ❷ Well-regarded Italian. Extensive menu. Caters for children. *Avenida de las Playas, Puerto del Carmen.*

JJ's £ ❸ Friendly family-orientated pub offering live music, karaoke nights, quiz nights and half-price drinks for ten minutes in every hour. *Calle Nicaragua 2, Puerto del Carmen.*

Iguaden ££ ❹ A very popular eating-house, with foreigners and tourists early in the evening and locals later. *Tias N. of Puerto. Tel: 928 524 047. Open daily 1200–midnight*

Restaurante El Guanche ££ ❺ A warm welcome awaits you here at this restaurant overlooking the sea. Fresh fish, meat and Canarian specialities. *Avenida de las Playas 88. Tel: 928 510 678.*

Sports Bar £ Popular for sports and football matches on TV. Serves English and Mexican food. Children's menu. *Puerto del Carmen.*

NIGHTLIFE

The Casino is open from 1100 with amusement arcade and snack bar. The gaming rooms open from 2000 to 0400 and offer American roulette and Black Jack. You must be 18 years and over and don't forget your passport! *Avenida de las Playas, C.C. Pequeña Europa 12. Tel: 928 515 000.*

The best bars and discos are on the main strip, the Avenida de las Playas. Check out the very popular Waikiki Beach Club, also The Big Apple, Hippodrome and Charlie's – open until at least 0300 . . .

 TIP! Trade in your old paperbacks at Bookswap, Calle Timanfaya 4.

Ex-pat bar owner in Puerto del Carmen

Playa de los Pocillos –
excellent family beach

On the eastern edge of Puerto del Carmen, the huge sandy expanse of Playa de los Pocillos has a lovely, quiet disposition. The name of the resort means 'Puddle Beach', but don't be put off! – Lanzarote has the lowest rainfall of all the Canarian Islands. It's simply a reference to the fact that high tides cover large areas of the beach by night, then ebb away to leave large patches of water to evaporate by day in the hot Lanzarote sun.

It is one of the top ten beaches of the whole island, quieter and less crowded than its sister beach of Playa Grande and popular with local families too. The promenade has been widened and beautifully landscaped and the paths and walkways decorated with shrubs and bushes, bordered with low walls of volcanic stone. Although Puerto del Carmen is just down the road, Los Pocillos has its own disco, bars, restaurants and plenty of shops lining the main promenade, the Avenida de las Playas.

THINGS TO SEE AND DO

Mini-golf *
Try Mini-golf San Antonio – just the place for all the family and friends – enjoying fantastic sea views. *Avenida de las Playas 80. Tel: 608 011 357. Open daily 1030–2300.*

Mega Fun Quad Bikes *
Quad Drive Lanzarote offers daily trips all over the island. Discover scenic forest tracks that can only be explored in quad vehicles. *C.C. Costa Mar, Local 20. Tel: 928 512 893.*

INDEPENDENT EXCURSIONS

The resort is on the coastline of Tías Municipality, one of the island's seven regions. This is home to a people whose individuality has been moulded by a combination of history, the rigours of a harsh climate and the island's volcanic origins. The true identity of the typical Lanzarotean can be found nearby in the villages of Conil, Mácher, La Asomada, La Geria – famous for its vineyards – Tegoyo and Tías itself. Generations of these inhabitants have survived difficult times by loyally clinging to their beliefs, traditions and their past way of life. All are easily accessible by car – ask your holiday representative for details of car hire or organised trips.

BEACHES

Playa de los Pocillos has a huge stretch of fine golden sands and the water is crystal clear. The calm, silky waters here make it an excellent place for inexperienced windsurfers to gain their confidence.

RESTAURANTS AND BARS

 The Bodegon ££ Patronised by locals and tourists alike. Each floor provides something different. *Opposite the church in the old town. Reservations advisable. Tel: 928 515 265.*

 Canayma Bar £ Cocktail bar with tropical atmosphere with salsa, *merengue*, cumbia, etc. *C.C. Costa Mar 1. Tel: 028 515 380. Closed Mon.*

 Chino Canton ££ Chinese restaurant specialising in Cantonese cuisine with a great selection of vegetarian dishes. Wonderful sea views from the terrace. *C.C. La Penita, Local 18 (2nd floor). Tel: 928 512 044.*

 Groucho Pub £ Great music. Darts. Plenty of *tapas* served by José and Curro. Satellite TV. *C.C. Costa Luz 22–24. Tel: 928 511 241.*

 L'Italia Bella £ Authentic Italian pizzas and pasta. *C.C. Los Jameos, Local 84. Tel: 928 514 798. Open 0900–midnight.*

 The Wishing Well £ Family-run British eatery with good home cooking. Full English menu featuring traditional Sunday roast lunch. *C.C. Costa Luz, Local 11.*

 The Tapas Tree £ Good bar food. *In Montana Tropical. Tel: 630 754 135.*

JUST FRIENDS

The usual greeting between friends and acquaintances is the double kiss where you touch cheeks first on the right then on the left. If one of the locals takes a liking to you, it would be rude not to reciprocate. When in Lanzarote . . . !

Matagorda – windsurfer's paradise

With a transfer time of just ten minutes from the airport, Matagorda is the most easily accessible of all Lanzarote's beach resorts. Playa de los Pocillos adjoins it, so making it the furthest beach in the Puerto del Carmen area. Where once it was a completely separate little village from Puerto del Carmen, it is now really a tasteful extension of the whole area, boasting an excellent natural, sandy beach and is regarded as a windsurfer's paradise.

It also has a good selection of shops, bars and restaurants, including the Cristobal Colón restaurant, (*see page 42*), one of the best in all the Canary Islands. If the pace is too relaxed, there's a greater variety of nightlife easily reached in Puerto del Carmen and Arrecife, the capital, is close at hand for shopping too.

THINGS TO SEE AND DO

Fishing **
If you fancy playing the part of Ernest Hemingway for a day and hunting marlin, Lanzamarlin offers fishing charters and excursions for big Atlantic fish including shark, barracuda, swordfish and wahoo as well. *Based at Puerto Calero. Tel: 629 078 206.*

Puerto Calero **
To the west is one of Europe's truly beautiful marinas in a magnificent setting, located on the main island road between Puerto del Carmen and Yaiza. The island's most celebrated present-day architect, Luis Ibáñez Margalef, was responsible for drawing up the plans for this new marina – literally blasted out of the rocks – and probably the finest of its kind on the island. A huge selection of bars with terraces and restaurants overlook the harbour.

Sailing on a catamaran***

From Puerto Calero you could treat yourself to a day aboard a catamaran with Catlanza S.L., possibly accompanied by dolphins; you might even spot whales or flying fish as you sail across via Puerto del Carmen to the famous beaches of Papagayo (*see page 47*). *Catlanza S.L. is based at Local, 1 Puerto Calero. Tel: 928 513 022.*

Submarine safaris **

Also departing from Puerto Calero daily from 0900 to 1900 are submarine safaris aboard the *Sub Fun 3* where you can experience the natural under-water world in a real submarine. *Puerto Calero, Local 2. Tel: 928 512 898.*

BEACHES

In contrast to other beaches in the Puerto del Carmen area, Matagorda benefits from breezes, making it excellent for windsurfing. The beach is sometimes almost completely covered at high tide. The windsurfing school is on the beach and has boards for hire.

RESTAURANTS

 Casa Gallega O'Orreo ££ Specialising in barbecued steaks, flambés, fish and live lobsters, spider crabs and shellfish daily. *Commercial Centre, Los Jameos, Local 62. Tel: 928 511 852.*

Cristobal Colón £££ An award-winning restaurant, regarded as one of the best in the Canaries. Mostly French cuisine including excellent fresh fish and a seven-course gastronomic menu in elegant surroundings with an outside terrace. Extensive wine list and impeccable service – just right for that special occasion. It's also only ten minutes' drive from the centre of Puerto del Carmen. *47 Commercial Centre, Matagorda. Tel: 928 512 554. Open daily 0900–2300.*

Musical Pub £ Tropical and international cocktails in a friendly atmosphere with live music. Also offers breakfast and snacks. *Commercial Centre, Matagorda, Local 5. Tel: 928 511 445.*

Steve's Balti House ££ A well-frequented Indian restaurant in Los Pocillos, Matagorda. *Tel: 928 510 987. Open daily 1830–midnight.*

All the southern resorts benefit from the highest number of sunshine hours on the whole island and, unlike the other Canary Islands, remain virtually rain-free all year round. Any rain that does fall usually comes between December and February, with an average of just 16 days per year! The cooling breeze can be very deceiving so do take precautions against the hot African sun – especially if you're out on the water!

Playa Blanca –
paradise and parrots

Playa Blanca has only recently developed as a tourist resort and port for connections with Fuerteventura, and it retains much of its earlier fishing village character. It is a more tranquil resort than its nearest neighbour, Puerto del Carmen with some artificial beaches and probably the prettiest beach on the island at Papagayo. Camping with facilities is now permitted on a nearby beach.

The hub of activity is still the original fishing village, around which the resort has developed. Modern building has spread either side of the old centre and beyond the port, but Playa Blanca still retains an intimacy that the other main resorts have lost.

Shops, cafés and restaurants line the pedestrianised sea-front promenade, which overlooks the small, but pretty, beach – an ideal spot for sipping a coffee, or something stronger, and watching the world go by. When the spirit moves you, take a look at the activity in the port area and possibly have a sail or try your hand at one of the watersports on offer.

Playa Flamingo

From the seashore, through the shimmering heat haze, you should be able to make out the small, dark volcanic shape of Isla de Lobos and behind it the outline of Fuerteventura with its halo of pale, sandy beaches, nearly 7 miles (11km) away across the channel. Some people windsurf across the channel, whilst others are content to have a go – or watch others – in the safe, more protected waters here at the main beach, Playa Dorada. Playa Blanca is very well placed too for visiting Timanfaya National Park and all the sights of the southern half of Lanzarote. It's also very handy for the west coast and El Golfo where the volcanic *malpais* (badlands) meets the powerful Atlantic breakers.

Visit the tourist office, in the port terminal building, by the ticket offices, for a local map and bus timetable. *Open Mon–Fri 0900–1400 & 1500–1700, 0800–1400 summer.*

THINGS TO SEE AND DO

Boat trips from the port ***

César II cruises to Fuerteventura to visit the famous sand dunes, the Papagayo beaches and Isla de Lobos. The inclusive price includes a snack, lunch with wine, and watersports – but some watersports may incur an extra charge. The Pirate Cruise, on board the *Marea Errota* also sails from Playa Blanca daily at 1000 and at 1600 during summer, and is ideal for children and dolphin spotting: (*tel: 928 517 633*). Tickets can usually be booked through your holiday representative.

Ferry to Fuerteventura **

The two ferries *Volcán de Tindaya* and *Buganvilla* make five return trips a day each in winter and six in summer, so why not hop across the water to spend the day in Corralejo (*see page 92*) and visit the famous sand dunes.

BEACHES

The original and sandy central beach is easily accessible but the two main beaches involve a 10 to 15-minute walk in opposite directions. To the east of the port lies the golden sand beach of Playa Dorada. The shallow water here is protected from rough seas by breakwaters and a barrier separates watersports activity from the swimmers. Although artificial, delightful palm-fringed Playa Flamingo to the west is a sheltered family beach with light golden sand and a superb ambience.

However, sun-worshippers will probably head for the famous **Papagayo Peninsula**, boasting arguably the finest beaches on the whole of Lanzarote. Papagayo means 'parrot' and refers to the fact that this nature reserve is in the shape of a parrot's beak. Once a secret paradise, these beaches now attract plenty of visitors, even though you have to bump along dusty, unmade roads to find them. The first beach you come to, and the most easily accessible, is Playa de Mujeres – the name means 'Women's Beach' but this is a superb beach for everyone – not just bathing beauties! It has golden sandy, protected coves with great snorkelling opportunities off the rocks where you'll see

multi-coloured fish, perhaps even the resident dolphins and the odd parrot fish too! The main beach, Playa de Papagayo, is about 15 minutes' drive from the centre of Playa Blanca, on the southernmost tip of the island and is perhaps the prettiest of all. But other lovely sandy beaches backed by sandy cliffs include Playa de los Pozos and La Caleta (also known as Puerto Muelas) – the naturists' secluded favourite. All these 'parrot' beaches have little shade and some do not have bars or restaurants, so do go prepared!

A small access toll charge is payable per car for the Papagayo beaches.

RESTAURANTS AND BARS

For its size, there is no shortage of restaurants and bars in Playa Blanca. Many of the restaurants line the pedestrianised promenade, which is very atmospheric by night. Those in search of pub grub, karaoke, football on Sky TV and a more swinging atmosphere should head for the Punta Limones Commercial Centre, above the port. Most cafés and restaurants have a children's menu and are family friendly.

 Casa Pedro ££ A first-class fish restaurant. *Ave. de Las Playas 16, Playa Blanca. Tel: 928 517 022.*

 Angela's Pizza Place £ Really good value. On the left as you enter Playa Blanca. *Tel: 928 515 430. Open daily 1200–1600, 1800–2300.*

 La Bodega £££ Delicious tapas of the day, a large variety of good Spanish wine. *On the main road above Uga. Tel: 928 830 147.*

 Bar Playa Blanca £ New very successful (and very busy) Italian restaurant between the two roundabouts going out of Playa Blanca towards Yaiza. *La Tegala. Tel: 928 517 552*

 Mar de Plata ££ Mainly fish but also meat dishes and delicious desserts. Outside seating. *On the central promenade. Avenida Marítima 36. Tel: 928 517 745.*

 Popeye's £ Good English food including breakfast and pub entertainment. Terrace. *Punta Limones Commercial Centre. Tel: 928 517 906.*

 Portofino ££ New, very successful Italian restaurant between the two roundabouts heading out of Playa Blancs towards Yaiza. *Tel: 928 518 388. Open Tues-Sun 1900–0100.*

Costa Teguise –
five golden beaches

The most northerly of the resorts, Costa Teguise (pronounced 'Tegeezy' to rhyme with 'breezy'!) is a purpose-built development with four centrally placed beaches. Its size is masked by the convolutions of the coastline, which gives each sandy beach the feel of being a separate resort. Despite not having an original fishing village at its heart, it nevertheless feels intimate, with an upmarket air.

Orientation is the biggest problem. The resort does not have an obvious heart, but the area around the Pueblo Marinero, in the southern corner of Las Cucharas beach, makes a good focal point. There are enough shopping centres scattered around to keep shoppers busily engaged, even as far out as Las Cucharas, opposite the Los Zocos Apartments. A wide range of goods is on offer and the centres are usually a good mix of shops, bars and restaurants. Water enthusiasts might be tempted out to the nearby aquatic park; next door, golfers can play a round at the only golf course to be found on the two islands, although two more are underway in Playa Blanca.

THINGS TO SEE AND DO

Watersports **
- **Aguapark:** Aquatic park below the golf course. Pools, chutes and slides; medical centre; supermarket; lockers; restaurant; lifeguards. A good reduction for children aged 2–12. *Tel: 928 592 128. Daily 1000–1800.*

- **Calipso Diving School**: instruction, equipment for hire, licence courses. *Commercial Centre Nautical, Avenida de las Islas Canarias. Tel: 928 590 879. Open daily.*

● **Sport Away Lanzarote** – Cucharas Beach: windsurfing school. International instructors. *Commercial Centre, Puerto Tahiche. Tel: 928 590 731.*

Walking and biking *

● **Hot Bike**: mountain and road bikes, etc, for hire. Organised tours, jeep and bike safaris. *Avenida de las Islas Canarias. Tel: 928 590 304.*

● **Trax Bike Hire**: for a bike to be used further afield (mountain and road bikes). *Avenida de las Islas Canarias. Tel: 928 592 028. Open Mon–Sat.*

Golf ***

● **Club de Golf de Costa Teguise:** A must for golfers, and a world away from coastal activity, is the delightfully situated 18-hole par-72 golf course overlooking Costa Teguise. Clubs and cars for hire, plus restaurant and bar. Under new management. *Avenida del Golf. Tel: 928 590 512/591 656.*

BEACHES

All the beaches have golden sand, and most are cove-like, and so protected from Atlantic rollers. Playa Charcos is quieter than Las Cucharas which sees most of the action, especially windsurfing. The promenade behind Las Cucharas skirts garden areas, and pleasant cafés and restaurants are close to hand. Moving further along the coast, hidden from view behind the Hotel Teguise Playa yet close to the centre, the shallow waters of intimate Playa Jablillo are popular with families. Continue past here to Playa Bastian, an away-from-it-all beach, where palms enhance the relaxing ambience. A fifth beach, Playa del Ancla, lies nearer Arrecife.

EXCURSIONS

Costa Teguise is well placed to explore the north of the island. There are three main routes out of here, the northernmost road passes under a large white gate with a cross on it – not the entrance to a cemetery! Both gate and cross are the creations of César Manrique, Lanzarote's most famous son. This road leads out to the cactus fields at Guatiza near the extraordinary Jardín de Cactus (Cactus Garden) (*see page 69*). This road continues to Haría, the 'Valley of 1,000 Palms' (*see page 66*) where the locals claim that they have more palm trees here than anywhere else in the Canaries. Another road leads south to the capital, Arrecife (*see page 20*), just down the coast, whilst a third heads inland towards the old capital Teguise (*see page 65*), the northern beaches and the volcanoes. For organised tours, ask your representative. The top sights not to be missed are Jameos del Agua (*see page 68*), the mysterious underground volcanic tunnel with its beautiful clear lake, home of the unique tiny, blind white crabs; Mirador del Río (*see page 66*) – the fantastic viewpoint of the narrow strait between the main island and its little sister, Isla Graciosa; Cueva de los Verdes (Greens' Cave) (*see page 68*) for a hauntingly magical experience through part of one of the longest lava cave systems in the world.

SHOPPING

Explore the shopping opportunities in the various Commercial Centres situated around the resort or catch the No 2 bus to Arrecife (*see page 20*) for a real shopping spree.

Markets An interesting craft market is held every Friday from 1800, creating a lovely atmosphere in the Plaza Pueblo Marinero. Teguise Sunday Market (*see page 65*), when the streets of the usually sleepy town burst into a kaleidoscope of colour and bustle, is on everyone's must-do list. There is also a market at Playa Blanca, Sat 0900–1400.

RESTAURANTS AND BARS

Visitors have a whole array of restaurants and bars from which to choose. Most offer similar quality, service, price and menu, so it really boils down to personal preference. Self caterers will find 'take-away service' a common feature at many establishments. If you cannot make up your mind, head for El Boulevard, Los Zocos (*tel: 928 592 122*), where a selection of restaurants, in a tent-like structure, offer Tex-Mex, Spanish *tapas*, grills, pizzas and ice-creams.

Casa Blanca ££ Popular stylish venue. Unusual grill restaurant in the Jablillo area. International menu. *Calle las Olas 4. Tel: 928 590 155. Dinner only.*

Portobello ££ Excellent food and service. *Calle Las Chucharas. Tel: 928 590 241. Open Tues–Sun.*

 La Jordana £££ One of the best restaurants on the island. *Calle los Geranios. Tel: 928 590 328. Open Mon–Sat.*

 **LagOmar £££** For a special treat visit this out-of-town restaurant (close to Teguise) for delicious Canarian cuisine. Housed in Omar Sharif's romantic former holiday villa, before he lost it in a game of cards! *LagOmar, Nazaret, Teguise. Tel: 928 845 665.*

 El Patio £ Canarian and international. *Plaza Pueblo Marinero. Tel: 928 590 945. Open for lunch and dinner.*

 **La Provence ££** Tasty mix of Mexican, Italian, Spanish and Provençal dishes at this popular grill restaurant. *Avenida del Jablillo. Tel: 928 592 218. Open for lunch and dinner.*

 Sports Bar £ Very popular with sports lovers. Satellite TV. English food. Children's menu. *Avenida del Jablillo. Tel: 928 591 714.*

 **Tiananmen Restaurant ££** Very popular Cantonese Chinese with huge terrace. Specialises in crispy duck – also does take-away. *Avenida del Jablillo, Commercial Centre, Las Olas, Local 4 (opposite Oasis Lanz Club). Tel: 928 590 526.*

 Golf Club ££ Very congenial surroundings for a mid-day snack. *Tel: 928 540 512. Open daily but not evenings.*

NIGHTLIFE

Check out the **Robinson Beach Club** for great tropical cocktails and the **Columbus Tavern Pub** – an English pub serving *tapas* with live music and satellite TV. Both are located in the Commercial Centre, Las Cucharas.

Opposite: Playa Jabillo

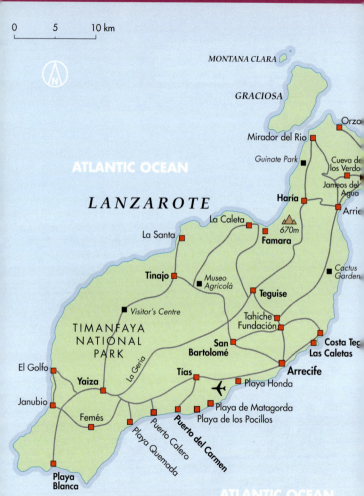

0   5   10 km

MONTANA CLARA

GRACIOSA

Orzo

Mirador del Rio

ATLANTIC OCEAN

Guinate Park

Cueva de los Verde

Jameos del Agua

LANZAROTE

Haría

Arrie

La Caleta

670m

La Santa

Famara

Tinajo

Museo Agricolá

Cactus Garden

Teguise

Visitor's Centre

TIMANFAYA NATIONAL PARK

Tahiche Fundación

Costa Teg

Las Caletas

San Bartolomé

La Geria

Arrecife

El Golfo

Yaiza

Tías

Playa Honda

Janubio

Femés

Playa de Matagorda

Playa de los Pocillos

Puerto Calero

Puerto del Carmen

Playa Quemada

Playa Blanca

ATLANTIC OCEAN

Timanfaya National Park

Recent volcanic activity on Lanzarote has left a corner of this island with a unique and spectacular landscape which has been sensitively protected as a National Park. Fiery crimson-hued mountains rise from *malpaís* (black cinders) in a state of harmonious disorder which only nature can create.

On the first day of September in 1730, between nine and ten at night, eyewitness Don Andrés Lorenzo Curbelo, who was Yaiza's priest at the time, saw the earth split apart at a spot close to the village of Timanfaya. During that first night, an enormous mountain rose from the bowels of the earth, with flames shooting from its summit. Volcanic activity in the area continued on and off for more than five and a half years. Waves of molten rock rolled over the nearby villages, carrying on into the sea where thousands of fish, poached alive in the boiling waters, ended up floating on the steaming surface.

During this period an immense sea of lava covered one of the most fertile regions of the island. Many small villages and hamlets were lost, including Timanfaya itself, which gave its name to the park. Surprisingly, as few as 420 houses were destroyed and there were no casualties.

Left behind from all this activity was a jumble of volcanic cones, the main one towering up to 1,670ft (510m), as well as satellite cones, lava tubes and a huge lava field. This lunar landscape covers an area of almost 20 square miles (51 square kilometres), and is a spectacle to be seen nowhere else on the earth.

A third of the whole island, including 11 villages, was buried under the lava – an eruption unsurpassed in recorded history. Less than 100 years later, another eruption increased the existing number of volcanoes from 26 to 29. Roadside signs depicting 'fire devils' remind you that you are in this grand and eerily beautiful volcanic landscape where the Fire Mountain, although peaceful from the outside, is only slumbering. The first astronauts were shown photos of this lunar landscape to prepare them for the first moon flight! Today, life carries on as normal in the villages like Yaiza and Uga where the lava flow stopped – and, as a bonus, it's been discovered that the tiny pebbles of *picón* – black volcanic debris – are a great boon to agriculture as they retain all the moisture. You'll see it used time and again in gardens and where the vines grow, and it's proved so invaluable that it is now being sold to farmers on the other Canary Islands.

Environmental protection

In 1974, the whole area, one of the youngest volcanic landscapes on the planet, was declared a National Park. The problem of allowing access to the public, while still protecting the park from environmental damage, has been neatly solved. Access roads have been made for cars and buses and a car park at Islote de Hilario – named after a hermit who lived alone here with just a donkey as company for 50 years! Here you'll find the extraordinary El Diablo (Devil) Restaurant (*££; open daily 1200–1530*), another of César Manrique's glass and lava masterpieces which he designed in 1970. From the restaurant's glass-walled circle, you get a thrilling panorama of the sea beyond contrasting with the awesome volcanic terrain. The food and Lanzarote wines are excellent at El Diablo and, if you haven't already sampled them, do try the tasty *papas arrugadas* – literally 'wrinkly potatoes' – delicious local new potatoes cooked in their skins with plenty of rock salt until the water has completely boiled away, always served with red or green mojo, tyickal Canarian sauces. From here, car drivers transfer to the special park buses and are driven around a circuit which visits all the main features. A commentary is given in three languages, including English.

Parties are allowed to proceed around the circuit with their own coach and guide. Although the bus may pause briefly for photographs, no one is allowed to get off. It is illegal to step off the road at any point in the National Park, except in designated areas.

The 8-mile (13km) tour takes around 45 minutes. Various landmarks are pointed out along the way including Raven's Crater, the point of the first eruption which destroyed the village of Timanfaya. The aptly named Valley of Tranquillity was created when the volcanoes were at the height of their activity. Great columns of grains (pyroclasts) were emitted which settled like sand all over the landscape, smoothing all the bumps and hollows.

Volcanic heat for the barbecue

Walkers can join free guided tours and are allowed access to the park on two trails (*see page 116 for further details*).

BARBECUE

Visitors on an organised excursion can attend a barbecue which uses volcanic heat, provided by geothermal energy – meat and chicken are grilled daily over nothing more than a hole in the ground.

Geothermal energy

Once back at Hilario's Plate, demonstrations are given to show that geothermal activity continues just below the surface of the ground.

At a depth of just 33ft (10m) the temperature has been measured at 600°C. In one area, visitors are encouraged to feel the warmth of the red gravel. A park attendant removes the surface with a shovel to show the increase in temperature just inches below the surface. In a second demonstration, an attendant pushes dry vegetation down into a shallow hole. It invariably catches alight and burns vigorously within seconds.

The most dramatic event is saved until last. A bucket of water is poured into a tube set in the ground. The water is ejected high into the air as a column of steam within seconds.

Camel riding

A separate section of Timanfaya National Park lies along the road leading from Yaiza to Mancha Blanca, at the foot of the Montañas del Fuego (Fire Mountains). Here you will find a camel station, with a bar, souvenir shop and toilets. One of the best ways of exploring this extraordinary lunarscape is on camel back and the short rides (maximum 20 minutes) are very popular. Each animal carries two passengers strapped into wooden seats, one on either side. The camel train is then led up the steep sides of the volcano by a guide. But do bear in mind that they're known to the locals as 'kissing camels', so you'd be well advised not to wear too much perfume, or other scented potions, or you might be the object of unwanted attention! They can also be rather noisy and smelly with unbelievably bad breath – but it's still a novel way of admiring the spectacular scenery!

TIP! A Visitor's Interpretation Centre is located just south of Mancha Blanca, on the Yaiza road (*see page 73*). This is an excellent place to learn more about volcanoes.

Next page: Timanfaya camel rides

Opposite: **Timanfaya geyser**

Northern Lanzarote

Although not especially large, Lanzarote is packed with interest and even in this relatively short 56-mile (90km) day-long tour, there is a lot to see. Highlights are three of César Manrique's creations and the chance to walk down a lava tube.

Some of the sights can be visited on organised excursions, or you can tour by rented car – ask your holiday representative for details.

The tour starts and finishes at Costa Teguise but it can easily be joined from any resort on the island simply by taking the quickest route to Teguise, the first port of call.

Teguise

Founded in the 15th century and capital of the island until 1852, Teguise is graced by old-world colonial architecture. One fine example is the Palacio de Spinola facing on to the spacious main square opposite the church, Nuestra Señora de Guadalupe (also known as San Miguel). The palace, an official residence of the President of the Canaries, is open as a museum allowing the public a glimpse of its furnished rooms. *Open Mon–Fri 1000–1700 (1000–1530 summer) and Sat 1000–1600 (1000–1430 summer). Small charge.*

Churches and convents abound within the streets of sleepy Teguise although these are easily outnumbered by craft and souvenir shops and café-bars. Above the town is the Castillo de Santa Bárbara, built in a commanding position astride the old volcano of Guanapay. The castle guarded Teguise from pirate attacks back in the 16th century. Now it houses the Museum of the Canarian Emigrant. It tells the sad story of mass migration, following the destruction of prime growing areas of the island by volcanic activity in the 18th century. *Open Mon–Fri 1000–1700 (1000–1430 summer), Sat & Sun 1000–1600 (1000–1430 summer). Small charge.*

There is an abundance of bars and restaurants, the best including Ikarus, Patio del Vino and La Bodeguita (next to Ikarus) for tapas and local wine. The Sociedad at Nazaret is a must; cheap, cheerful and noisy!

Opposite: Mirador del Rio

Teguise welcomes the biggest market on the island on Sunday mornings, bringing the town to life with a festive atmosphere. The market is an Aladdin's Cave of delights in which local crafts feature prominently.

Haría

Mountainous scenery takes over on heading north to Haría. A high point is reached at the Mirador de Haría which offers interesting views of the road ahead snaking down towards Haría hidden amongst palm trees, known as the 'Valley of 1,000 palms'. Haría is a pleasing oasis for a quiet wander and, perhaps, a lunch break at one of the town's numerous restaurants and bars.

Mirador del Río

Continue north and, if you have children, consider diverting for the Tropical Park at Guinate (*see page 115*) before reaching Mirador del Río. Located on the northerly tip of the island, on the cliffs of Famara, this viewpoint overlooks Isla Graciosa and three tiny islets further out to sea. It is no ordinary viewpoint. In a natural hollow in the mountain, a large restaurant was constructed and then capped by two large soil-covered domes. A huge panoramic window gives views to the islands, but visitors can also absorb the scenery from outdoor platforms. *Open daily 1000–1745. Small entrance charge.*

Orzola

The return road from the Mirador follows the coast briefly and offers yet more enticing views over the islands. Turn left on rejoining the main route and head for Orzola. The most northerly town on the island, Orzola is a typical fishing village, well supplied with popular fish restaurants. Crowds gather when the fishing boats are landing their catches, especially when marlin or shark have been caught. Ferries to Isla Graciosa leave from here twice a day, weather permitting.

Do visit Las Pardelas, a farm with activities and a snack bar (English spoken). From Orzola there is a ferry that goes to a small unspoilt island called La Graciosa; ask your rep for times.

Opposite: Sheltered sands at Costa Teguise

Jameos del Agua

Return using the coastal road, driving through lava fields for a time, with views of alluring lagoons bordered by silver-white sand. Pick up signs for the not-to-be-missed Jameos del Agua, a captivating grotto of volcanic origin with an underground lake, now enhanced with restaurant, bars, showpiece pool, and exhibition gallery.

Nature had the first word in creating this volcanic tube when Mount Corona erupted 3,000 years ago, pouring out huge lava flows. When the lava eventually solidified on the surface, the liquid lava continued to flow inside, leaving a tunnel. Some parts collapsed in time leaving lava bubbles. César Manrique then came along to turn the system into a fantasy of caves and pools.

Visitors enter via a huge cavern, also used as a restaurant, and proceed through a section of tube with an underground lake. A small albino crab (*Munidopsis polimorpha*), easily seen on the dark rocks, lives in the lake. This leads to a decorative pool of azure-blue water with a startling white surround, the trade mark of César Manrique. The next surprise is a huge underground concert hall, which hosts cultural events on a regular basis. *Open daily 1100–1900 (July–Sept 0930–1845), also Tues, Fri and Sat nights 1900–2300.*

Afterwards head inland to the nearby Cueva de los Verdes.

Cueva de los Verdes

The 'Cave of the Greens' is not named after the conservation movement, but after the Green family who once used this cave as a home. Cueva de los Verdes is actually a section of lava tube which is part of a system of underground tunnels almost 4 miles (6km) long. Such tubes were formed by lava flows which solidified on the surface but continued to flow and drain beneath.

A guided tour takes visitors on a walk just over a mile long (2km) through the various galleries. It lasts about 50 minutes. Low and sometimes narrow passages make the going difficult for tall or large people and at least normal agility is required. *Open daily from 1000; last tour leaves at 1700.*

Jardín de Cactus

Proceeding southwards, there is just one more stop to make for the Cactus Garden designed as a work of art by César Manrique (*see page 8*). Under the guiding hand of César Manrique, a small quarry in the village of Guatiza was converted into a work of art with the aid of cacti. The impact of the design and layout of the garden strikes you immediately on entry. There are terraces to walk around to explore different viewpoints and 1,400 species to examine in detail. A gleaming white windmill forms the back-drop, and this is still used occasionally to grind *gofio* (toasted maize meal) on a commercial scale. *Open daily 1000–1745.*

RESTAURANTS

 Amanacer ££ One of the most popular restaurants on the island. Specialises in fish. Does not take bookings. *Main street in Arrieta.*

 El Lago ££ International restaurant serving fresh fish. Lobster pool, centrally located. Very popular, especially on Sundays. *Tel: 928 848 176. Open daily between Arrieta and Punta Mujeres on the coastal road.*

Central Lanzarote

This 75-mile (120km) full-day tour crosses the island to take in some of the sights and sounds of the northern coast. It is hard to escape César Manrique creations on this island and there are two more visited on this tour. These are his own home and the Monumento al Campesino, his monument to farmers. Other reminders of Manrique are the huge, often colourful, mobiles dominating roundabouts, usually encountered when least expected.

As a painter and sculptor, Manrique did all he could to turn Lanzarote, his native island, into a living example of his artistic beliefs, reflecting the natural volcanic beauty into the art and architecture of the country. It is largely thanks to him that the island's skyline is free of high-rise developments and advertising hoardings.

Some of the sights can be visited on organised excursions, or you can tour by rented car – ask your holiday representative for details.

Costa Teguise is the starting point but it is simple enough to join this tour from anywhere on the island. Just head for the first stopping point, the Fundación César Manrique on the San Bartolomé–Tahiche road. The village of San Bartolomé has been transformed in recent years and is worth a stop, perhaps to visit the new museum 'Tanit'. Where once the villagers used mules and camels as their means of transport, now they're more likely to be seen in smart four-wheel drives. But the centre of this now prosperous little community is still the small square in front of the pretty whitewashed church. In the surrounding little alleys, you can see (and buy) the typical straw hats plaited by hand by the village women.

From Costa Teguise, leave by the road which passes the golf course. Continue over the roundabout with the towering silver mobile to reach the Fundación César Manrique.

Opposite: Fundación César Manrique

The Fundación César Manrique

César Manrique built for himself a most unusual house which incorporates his own distinctive artistry into imaginative architecture. This two-storey building incorporates five lava bubbles formed from earlier volcanic activity. Outside it might seem relatively traditional with its characteristic dazzling white contrasting with jet black lava, if you ignore for the moment distinctive features like the colourful mobile, reminiscent of a child's enormous toy and the long whitewashed wall adorned with a lavishly painted vibrant mural.

Inside it is very different. Each of the lava bubbles has been made into a distinctive room – one with a palm tree growing up through the roof, another with a trickling fountain – and stunning views out on to the lava fields. The blue and white swimming pool built into a collapsed lava tube and the 'snow' tunnels connecting the 'igloo' bubbles are all especially memorable.

For culture buffs, the art gallery is a must, featuring Manrique's own powerful canvasses complemented by works of most of the top names of 20th-century modern and abstract art, including Tapies, Picasso and Miró.

César Manrique gave his house over to a private foundation which now runs it for the benefit of all. Above all, this was a house designed to be lived in – not just a museum to be visited – where the architecture is always brilliant, great fun and sometimes truly astonishing! The foundation has a bookstore, shop, café and car park. *Open Mon–Sat 1000–1800, Sun 1000–1500 (1 July–31 Oct daily 1000–1900).*

La Caleta de Famara **

Return to the silver mobile and take the road to Teguise (*see page 65*). Turn left there towards Mozaga and right shortly to cross the plains to La Caleta de Famara. This small fishing village looks on to the huge sweep of sand dunes in the Bay of Famara, foaming under crashing rollers that are greatly loved by surfers. The golden sandy beaches and dunes are popular with naturists too. But the north-westerly wind makes the ocean currents potentially dangerous, so swimming and diving are discouraged and it's definitely not the place for novice windsurfers! This is the village where César Manrique spent his childhood and the mountains of white foam here might have been the inspiration behind the strong white influence in his creations. There are good views out towards Isla Graciosa, framed by the Famara cliffs.

Museo Agrícola El Patio **

Leave La Caleta by the road to Soo and look out for the windmills just before Tiagua. These belong to the Museo Agrícola El Patio, a rural life museum, whose themes are antiquity, tradition and history. Seeing mattresses stuffed with banana leaves might make you thankful for modern times. The excellent museum has plenty to absorb, from 'blood mills' to 101 uses for *gofio* (toasted maize meal). Better still, it finishes with a wine tasting! There is a pleasant bar on site. *Open Mon–Fri 1000–1730, Sat 1000–1430. Closed Sun. Admission charge.*

Take the road for Tinajo and turn north for La Santa. Follow the road around to drive on to La Isleta, passing the La Santa sports complex, a time-share complex famous for the high standard of its sports facilities. Drive around the islet, well equipped with stopping places to watch surfers, and back on to the main road.

Head back south via Tinajo to Mancha Blanca and take the road through the National Park towards Yaiza. This leads past the Timanfaya Visitor Centre, which is well worth a stop.

Timanfaya Visitor's Centre **

Airily designed with halls on different levels, this centre is formulated to help you interpret the volcanic landscape of the National Park, as well as the flora and fauna. There are plenty of hands-on exhibits, including touch-screen computers that allow visitors to choose their own pathways through the information. An audio-visual programme about the National Park, lasting 30 minutes, is presented repeatedly. Headphones are required for the commentary in English.

One of the highlights is the Eruption Hall, where volcanic eruptions are simulated, complete with very realistic sounds, smells and vibrations. There is a shop selling handicrafts and books about the park. *Open daily 0900–1900. Admission free.*

Fire mountains and lava fields dominate the scenery down to Yaiza and from there it is back to Mozaga by the La Geria road for a final stop at the Monumento al Campesino (*see page 24*), which marks the geographical centre of the island, and which was designed by Manrique as a tribute to the island's farmers.

RESTAURANTS

 Las Bajas £ Popular restaurant which offers a good selection of fish and meat dishes at prices unlikely to frighten tourists away. *Calle Callejón, La Caleta de Famara. Tel: 928 528 617.*

 Casa Ramon £ Simple fried fish, *paella* or pasta in authentic bar-restaurant. *Calle Callejón, La Caleta de Famara.*

Timanfaya National Park

La Era ££ Housed in a group of 17th-century farm buildings, this is one of the island's most famous restaurants. Local dishes are a speciality; expect to pay a little more, but worth it. The white Malvasia wine really is a home product. *Carretera General, Yaiza. Tel: 928 830 016. Open 1300–2300.*

La Geria

Southern Lanzarote

The southern part of Lanzarote has its fair share of attractive fishing villages, beautiful beaches and dramatic coastline. The green lagoon of El Golfo is one of the highlights of this tour but so is the garden city of Yaiza. The best is saved until the last. The drive through the wine-growing district of La Geria reveals landscapes unrivalled on the island. Allow a full day for this 70-mile (112km) tour.

Some of the sights can be visited on organised excursions, or you can tour by rented car – ask your holiday representative for details.

Puerto del Carmen is the starting point selected for this tour but it is easily joined from the other major resorts on the island. Leave Puerto del Carmen by the road to Mácher. Look for the track off left to Puerto Calero, immediately following the roundabout, which provides a direct route to Puerto Calero.

Puerto Calero

Highly regarded as a marina, the quality of the boats moored here hints at an upmarket character. Gleaming white, the harbour-front has its fair share of cafés and restaurants. Puerto Calero offers a variety of sea trips, including a submarine excursion, and watersports. Sail and motor boats are also available for hire. (See pages 41/42).

Playa Quemada

Playa Quemada is the next destination but this cannot be reached without going back first to the main road. The small village of white cube houses overlooks a rocky shoreline. There is an adjoining beach of black sand, but without facilities. It has one or two good restaurants including the '7 Islas' where you can tackle fresh lobster at reasonable prices.

Femés

Return to the main road and watch very shortly for the left turn off to Femés. This small town is perched on a high saddle at the foot of the Atalaya mountain. It provides great views down to the coast and is one of the best places on the island to view the sunset. Continue through Femés to rejoin the road into Playa Blanca, one of the island's major resorts (*see page 44*). East of Playa Blanca are the natural and unspoilt beaches of Papagayo. They can be reached by car – part of the road is unsurfaced and dusty, though not particularly rough.

Janubio salt pans

When leaving Playa Blanca, take the old road to Yaiza from the roundabout (the exit past the new road) which runs parallel with the new road for much of the way but passes close to the old salt pans at Janubio. Salt is still

LANZAROTE VINEYARDS

Farming entirely in volcanic ash, the farmers of La Geria scoop out hollows in which to plant their vines. These hollows are protected by *zocos* (semicircular walls). The patterns produced dignify an already unearthly landscape. No irrigation is used but the vines survive on moisture absorbed by the pumice-like stone at night.

produced here, but production has declined through falling demand. Sea water is pumped into small square pans and allowed to evaporate. The salt is gathered into heaps to dry further in the sun before removal.

El Golfo

Turn left from the old road to head around the salt pans to reach the shore. Stop at La Hervideros to watch the sea thundering up the cliffs. Carry on and take the first road off to Charco de Los Clichos which gives a view of the green lagoon from sea level or carry on to the north side of the village of El Golfo. A few minutes' walk up the hill out of the village of El Golfo gives a view down on the diminishing emerald-green waters of the lagoon trapped between ochre cliffs and black sands. The small village itself spreads along the sea edge providing opportunities to dine right at the edge of the sea.

La Geria

Return from El Golfo directly to Yaiza, which is colourfully gardened along its highways and one of the prettiest villages on the island. It is worth stopping for a moment for a wander around. From Yaiza take the La Geria road through the wine-growing area. Farming on arid volcanic clinker, the farmers have tamed the land in their own unique style and added their own artistry to an already unusual landscape. There are a number of *bodegas* in La Geria offering wine tasting. El Grifo Bodega, with its wine museum, is one of the most interesting to visit. *Tel: 928 520 500. Open daily 1030–1800. Entrance free.*

The La Geria route ends at Mozaga. Turn right, back towards Arrecife and Puerto del Carmen.

El Golfo

RESTAURANTS

 Costa Azul ££ A sea-front fish restaurant, rustic but pleasant. The daily special is particularly good value. *El Golfo. Tel: 928 173 199. Closed Sun.*

 Restaurant El Campo ££ Both Canarian and international cuisine on offer. Located just before the football field in Yaiza. *Tel: 928 830 344. Open 0900–2300.*

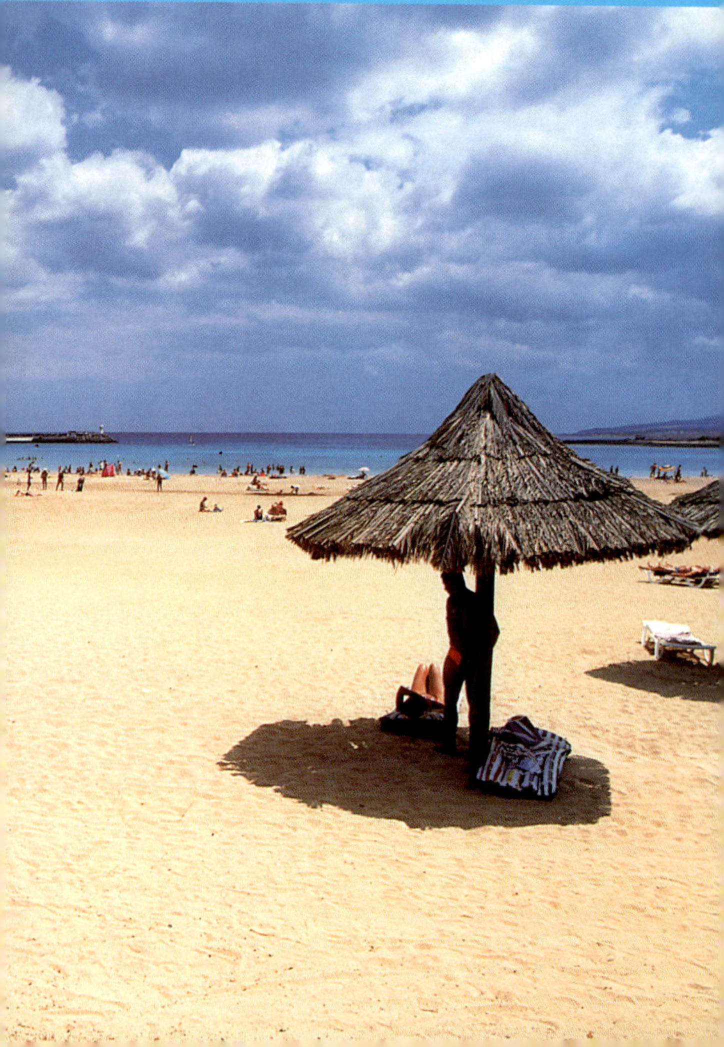

Caleta de Fuste (El Castillo) –
golden sandy beach

Life in this relaxing family resort revolves around the beach, the port and El Castillo Commercial Centre. While most of the resort lies close to the coast, there has been some extension west of the main road. The two are linked by a mini-train which runs frequently to a well-advertised timetable.

The beach, a deep curve of golden sand, enjoys some protection from the worst excesses of the Atlantic rollers and is popular with families. The resort is great too for windsurfers and watersports enthusiasts. There are several shopping centres to explore: some are lively by day, offering a good mix of shops, bars and restaurants, while others come to life more during the evening and are the best places for nightlife.

Looking inland, the conical hill nearby is known locally as 'chipmunk' hill and is a popular excursion for those prepared to walk. Commonly called chipmunks, the small, almost friendly animals that live on this hill and gave it its name are, in fact, ground squirrels introduced from North Africa.

Both the Caleta de Fustes beach and El Castillo owe their names to the fact that in olden days a *fuste* (light vessel for exploration) was at anchor there, permanently at the service of the island. The 18th century *castillo* (castle/watchtower) is now part of the holiday complex that bears its name. It stands next to a little pleasure harbour with restaurants, bars and water-sports hire facilities and is a great place to watch the fishing boats arrive.

TIP! Caleta de Fuste has one of the best candle shops on the islands. Go and watch them being made. If you are tempted to buy some of these colourful candles, they are well packed for travelling.

THINGS TO SEE AND DO

Boat trip **
At the harbour you can take a boat trip to Pozo Negro, just south of Caleta de Fuste. The boat does not put you ashore, but you can spend a magical hour snorkelling in the crystal clear waters. Contact your representative for more details.

Chipmunk Hill ***
A well-worn path leads up the hill behind the resort where the 'chipmunks', or ground squirrels, can be seen. Be prepared for quite a stiff climb. Start out by taking the mini-train to its inland terminus. From here the hill is clearly visible, as is the upward route. The animals are getting used to being fed, so many have lost their nervousness in the presence of humans. These ground squirrels were introduced from North Africa as a single pair in 1965. Since then they have multiplied to become one of the commonest animals on the island. There is a good colony living on this hill.

Tennis **
The tennis courts by the beach are available to non-residents; enquire at the kiosk.

Windsurfing **
Caleta de Fuste offers the opportunity for beginners to take lessons in windsurfing or for experienced surfers to enjoy the sport. Contact the Fanatic Fun Centre Wind Surfing School at the harbour. *Tel: 928 535 999. Open 1000–1700, or longer if conditions are good.*

Opposite: Camel safari

SHOPPING

Great excitement attends the arrival of the market every Saturday morning. Stalls lying dormant throughout the week spring to life selling a great range of clothing, crafts and souvenirs. It's the same selection of stalls that go to Corralejo on Mondays and Fridays.

EXCURSION

Puerto del Rosario

Just over 7 miles (12km) north lies the island's capital (the no 3 bus goes via the airport daily every hour, on the half-hour, except during siesta time!). Originally known as Puerto de Cabras (Goat's Port) – a reference to the fact that there are more goats per head than inhabitants on Fuerteventura! – it was later changed to the more romantic Puerto del Rosario (of the Rosary). Today the harbour is the most important on the island, and the city is home to around 80 per cent of the population. For clothes shopping you will find this the best option on the island. Why not also try the delicious *queso de cabra* (soft white goat's cheese) to remind you of the origins of the city? There are plenty of bars and restaurants around the harbour also offering *el cocido* – Fuerteventura's typical meat and chickpea stew.

RESTAURANTS AND BARS

Choice is something diners are not short of in this resort. Visitors quickly find their own favourites but here are a few starting suggestions.

 Cavern Sixties Bar £ Live 60s music every night. *Near to Puerto Restaurant Castillo in the Muelle Deportivo.*

 Heinken Hard Music £ Soul and blues. Approximately 90 different beers. *Leon y Castillo 146. Tel: 670 844 277. Open Mon–Sat 1100–0300, Sun 1700–0300.*

 **O Fado ££** Good, hearty Portuguese food is on offer at this moderately priced restaurant. Dine on the balcony to the sound of live music. Try the roast goat or perhaps choose a good steak, although there is plenty of fish on offer. *Castillo Centre. Tel: 928 163 369.*

 **La Frasquita ££** Overlooking the sea, this restaurant serves fresh fish at reasonable prices. *Muelle Deportivo. Open for lunch and dinner.*

Puerto Castillo Restaurant ££ A little more expensive than others in the resort but definitely one for that special treat. Choose from a balanced menu between fish and meat and dine in style with a great view of the harbour. *Muelle Deportivo. Tel: 928 163 100. Open 1800–2300.*

 Don't be surprised if you see members of the Foreign Legion on traffic duty! The Spanish Foreign Legion has its headquarters at Puerto del Rosario and you may well see these tough, macho soldiers when they're not out on manoeuvres in the desert.

Playa Jandía –
spectacular sands

A magnificent stretch of sand is the inspiration behind the development of Jandía into one of the most popular resorts on the island.

The Jandía peninsula, along the south-eastern coast of the island, has 20 miles (32km) of vast pale sands and unspoiled beaches lapped by aquamarine waters. It is a mecca for windsurfers and the annual World Windsurfing Championships are held at Sotavento, just north of Jandía Playa in July/August where wind speeds can reach up to force 9.

Good accommodation, lively shopping centres, amusement arcades and modern facilities contrast with the old-world atmosphere of Morro Jable, the characterful fishing village lying next door. This is the southernmost resort of the Jandía peninsula and, as well as its delightful Spanish appeal, it has a very pleasant promenade by the town beach with a wide choice of cafés, bars and especially good fish restaurants.

The tourist office in Jandía is to be found at the Shopping Centre, Morro Jable. *Tel: 928 540 776.*

THINGS TO SEE AND DO

SM Zoo and Park *
Lying at the northern end of Jandía, this zoo has a selection of birds and animals to see including birds, monkeys and crocodiles. Admission charge. *Tel: 928 161 135. Open 0900–1930.*

Watersports ***
Jandía offers good opportunities for all sorts of watersports – ask your holiday representative for details. Windsurfers are catered for at the centre near Club Robinson. Water-skiing is also available from Jandía Water Sports

on the beach. Scuba divers need to contact Club de Felix. *Tel: 928 541 418. Open daily 0900–1900. Closed Sat in winter. Catamaran hire (2 boats) is available between 1000 and 1530. Tel: 928 735 656.*

BEACHES

The long, golden and empty beaches of all Fuerteventura – especially in the south – are superb and far better than the gritty volcanic type found elsewhere in the Canaries. Black beaches here are very rare. Jandía's spacious beach, of golden white sand, is separated from the road by a stretch of scrub which is protected from development. It is criss-crossed by footpaths, all of which lead eventually on to the sands. Semicircular wind-breaks of dark volcanic stone at the rear of the beach provide shelter for sunbathers on days when the breeze is strong. Some areas on the beach have sunbed facilities but there is more than enough space to find a private corner to pitch a towel.

RESTAURANTS AND BARS

Playa Jandía sunset

 Rico Rico £
International fare. *Centro Commercial, Playa Paradiso. Tel: 928 540 457. Open daily 11.30–2300.*

 El Dorado £
Breakfast and lunch only. Canarian food. *Calle Senora del Carmen 31, Morro Jable. Tel: 928 540 336. Closed Sunday.*

 Clavijo £ Very busy restaurant serving international fare. *Avenida, Morro Jable. Open Mon–Sat 1130–2230.*

Costa Calma – calm and beach

The sheltered southern coast has the finest beach in the whole of the Canaries. Two resorts have developed at either end of this 15-mile (25km) stretch of sand – Costa Calma at the northern end and Jandía at the southern. Here the beautiful sands are backed by low cliffs and a scattering of coves and rocks gives the beach a huge amount of character, perhaps more so than the seemingly endless stretches further south.

As tranquil as the name suggests, Costa Calma is a family resort facing on to a huge sweep of golden white sand. It started originally as a private venture before tourism investment was encouraged. Elegant houses now mingle with hotels, apartments and commercial centres. These have developed in separate areas spanning the main road, which leaves some wandering on foot to reach the various parts.

Interest in this resort focuses largely on the pleasures offered by the extravagant sweep of sandy beach backed by low cliffs and the Sotavento Commercial Centre. Commercial Centres on these islands mean more than shopping centres – they offer a rich mix of bars, restaurants and shops. This is true here and the C.C. Sotavento offers a good selection of restaurants and bars which come to life during the evening. Although the resort is not so large, there are shops enough to buy everything from surfing clothes, cameras and electrical goods, to ladies fashions, watches, jewellery and perfumes.

The no 5 bus runs hourly, on the half-hour, (*Mon–Sat 0930–2130*) down to Jandía where you can enjoy the facilities of Costa Calma's neighbouring resort and explore the adjacent fishing village of Morro Jable.

THINGS TO SEE AND DO

Boat trips **

Sail aboard the catamaran *Magic* along the coast of Costa Calma enjoying the stunning views. You'll have the opportunity to swim and enjoy some watersports together with a buffet lunch served with wine, beer and soft drinks. Or, leaving from Morro Jable, you could sail aboard the *Maxi* towards the lighthouse of Jandía. As this is a sailing boat guests are welcome to help the crew throughout the day – hoisting sails, steering – or just relaxing as you sail around the southern tip of the coastline. For further details of boat trips, see your holiday representative.

Gran Tarajal and Tarajalejo *

Just up the coast the beaches of Gran Tarajal and Tarajalejo, with their fine black sand, are unique in the island – as are the palm trees of this area, especially in the Valley of Gran Tarajal where a flourishing plantation of date palms grow. The leaves and stems provide material for handiwork, like basket weaving and the typical *majorero* straw hat, a real symbol of the island and its people. Gran Tarajal is an easy drive away on Fuerteventura's uncrowded roads.

RESTAURANTS AND BARS

 Restaurante Averida Italia ££ Extensive Italian menu. *Ave. Paco Hierro, Gran Tarajal. Tel: 928 162 209. Open daily 1130–2400.*

 Restaurante Victor ££ Local food and fresh fish. *Juan Soler 1, Tel: 928 870 910. Open Tues–Sun 1200–1700.*

 **Posada San Borondón £** Spanish bar oozing with atmosphere. Cured hams drape from the ceiling and a selection of local cheeses are on offer. Tuck into a cold meat platter while testing out the Dorada beer. *C.C. Sotavento.*

 **Bar Restaurante Clavijo £** Cheap, cheerful and noisy. *On the main road from Tarajelejo towards Gran Tarajal (approx. 10km). Tel: 928 174 299.*

 Windsurfing is a popular sport here in Costa Calma and there is an opportunity to hire equipment and for beginners to take lessons. Contact the Fanatic Fun Centre on the beach.

SHOPPING

The best shops are found in the Commercial Centre on Avenida de los Delfines. Try **Toy Regalos** for toys, **Tot Musica** for everything musical, **Alba** for perfume, **Lladró** for china.

Fuertaventura's Costa Calma

Corralejo – top resort and dazzling dunes

Originally a fishing village, Corralejo has developed into the major resort on the island. A touch of old Spain can still be found in the centre, with good shopping and water activities never far away. Its greatest claim to fame is its close proximity to a magnificent 6.2-mile (10km) stretch of bleached sand beach and dunes.

During the day, local life in Corralejo centres around the port area, where the ferry departs daily to Lanzarote and boats make trips out to the Isla de Lobos.

Close to the port lies the old centre, quiet by day but atmospheric by night. Here is the chance to capture the magic of Spain by dining in the old square (Plaza Felix Estévez – also known as 'Music Square') to the sound of a guitar or by the wave-lapped shore close by. If your preference is for small and intimate then this is the area to explore.

Shops crowd the narrow streets in the old quarter then spill out along Avenida del General Franco. The evening buzz continues along this avenue where there is a wide choice of goods on display as well as a further selection of bars and restaurants.

Whilst many visitors are content to loll around their apartment pool, the lure of wild, untamed landscapes tempts many others to trek out to the nearby sandy beaches and dunes. The dunes just behind Corralejo are the largest and most impressive single area of dunes in the whole of Fuerteventura, reminiscent of a miniature Sahara. As well as sun-worshippers, you'll find a lot of windsurfers here. These spectacular beaches are framed by great hills of dazzling sand and they also support unusual types of plants that can only thrive in these salty, dry sands. You'll also find they're very popular with nudists, as well as windsurfers – not to mention nudist windsurfers!

 The tourist office in Corralejo is to be found at the Plaza Grande de Corralejo. *Tel: 928 866 235. Open Mon–Fri 0800–1400. Closed Sat and Sun.*

THINGS TO SEE AND DO

Cycling *
The countryside immediately surrounding Corralejo is relatively flat and there are tracks, especially out towards La Oliva, suitable for off-road cycling.

Mini-tren ***
Try the local beaches of Galera and Waikiki, or head out to the desert-like dune area on the Mini-Tren (Mini-Train). The train runs every half an hour from 0900 starting near the port before trundling its way as far as Agujas on the edge of the dunes. To head further into the dunes, catch the bus or take a taxi as far as the Oliva Beach Hotel. There are refreshment kiosks at intervals along the shore.

Watersports **
There are plenty of opportunities to enjoy watersports. Conditions nearly always favour windsurfing but there are also pedalos, and other forms of watersport. These are available from the harbour area, the small beaches in town or the sand dunes near Oliva Beach Hotel.

Opposite: Corralejo sand dunes

SHOPPING

The market comes to town every Monday and Friday where you can buy anything from fake Gucci watches to carved elephants. A lot of the stallholders are African and they do a great trade in hair braiding. *Calle Principal, opposite the Hotel Lobos Bahía from 0900 to 1400.*

EXCURSIONS

Isla de Lobos ***

A real desert island, only a 15-minute boat ride away, Isla de Lobos takes its name from the seals that once lived here. The island is small, with the greatest coast to coast distance of just over 2 miles (3.5km). It is dominated by the Montaña Lobos – once volcanic, which rises to an altitude of 417ft (127m). The whole island is now a protected zone as part of the Dune and Ocean Park of Corralejo. It is a great place to relax. The island has no roads, vehicles or inhabitants. There is a good beach with refreshment facilities, and footpaths allow you to wander around the island. It takes longer than you might expect, so allow 2–3 hours, depending on the heat. To get there ask your holiday representative for information about excursions, or take the regular ferry, M Y *Isla de Lobos,* which departs daily from Corralejo at 1015 and returns from Lobos at 1600. The glass-bottomed boat *El Majorero* departs at 1000 and 1200 except Wednesday.

Lanzarote ***

Take the 40-minute boat trip over to Playa Blanca (*see page 44*). An organised tour is the best option to pack most visits into one day. Tours typically visit the spectacular Timanfaya National Park (*see page 56*) to enjoy a unique volcanic experience and visit the La Geria wine-growing region to taste some of Lanzarote's own wines (*see page 78*). Some tours include Jameos del Agua, one of César Manrique's spectacular creations built in part of a lava tube (*see page 68*).

   If you want to travel independently, Lineas Fred Olsen and Naviera Armas SA both run regular services between Corralejo and Playa Blanca on Lanzarote. The Olsen ship, *Buganvilla,* leaves Corralejo daily at 0900, 1100, 1500, 1700, 1900, and returns from Playa Blanca at 0800, 1000, 1400, 1600 and 1800. A free bus service is offered by the Olsen line from Playa Blanca to Puerto del Carmen for the 0900 sailing. The bus returns from Puerto del Carmen at 1700 for the 1800 sailing. The *Volcán de Tindaya,* run by Naviera Armas, departs Corralejo daily at 0800, 1000, 1200 (not Sundays), 1400, 1800 and 2000 and returns from Playa Blanca at 1700 and 1900.

Lazy Daze

Sail the seas around Lanzarote, or relax on Papagayo beach (*see page 46*). Ask your representative for details.

Treasure Island

Cruise over to Los Lobos and relax on your own deserted island. Fun and games for everyone (*see opposite*). Ask your representative for prices and times.

RESTAURANTS AND BARS

 Chablis Wine Bar £ Relaxed, comfortable and reasonable. Serves breakfast and pub meals. *Avenida del General Franco.*

 Restaurante Averida ££ Good variety and excellent portions. Always busy. *General Prim, Corralejo. Tel: 928 867 145.*

 La Marquesina ££ Locals and tourists mix in this relaxed harbourside fish restaurant. *Muelle Viejo, Old Town Harbour. Tel: 928 535 435. Open all day.*

 La Rosa de Benti ££ An authentic Italian restaurant/pizzeria by the harbour where pizzas are cooked in a stone oven heated with wood. Half portions for children. *Calle La Iglesia. Tel: 928 867 618. Open for lunch and dinner.*

 Sotavento ££ Ideal for balmy days and nights on the sea-front. Good for fresh fish but also serves a selection of meat dishes. Children's menu. *Avenida Marítima 19. Tel: 928 536 417. Open for lunch and dinner.*

NIGHTLIFE

Sandpiper British Bar £ Features Sky Sports, English beers and ciders plus 1950s, 60s and 70s music. *Downstairs in Centro Comercial Altántico.*

Waikiki £ Open-air disco for the over-20s, tourists and locals. Spanish and English music. *Open 1800–0400. Free entrance.*

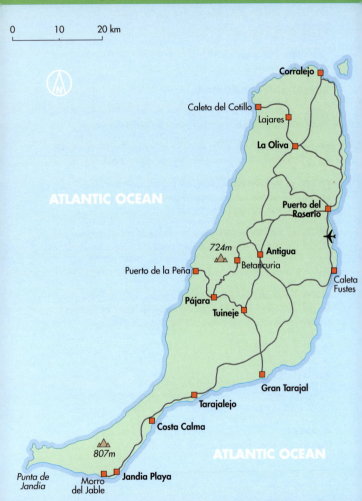

0   10   20 km

Corralejo

Caleta del Cotillo

Lajares

La Oliva

ATLANTIC OCEAN

Puerto del Rosario

724m

Antigua

Betancuria

Puerto de la Peña

Pájara

Tuineje

Caleta Fustes

Gran Tarajal

Tarajalejo

Costa Calma

807m

ATLANTIC OCEAN

Punta de Jandía

Morro del Jable

Jandía Playa

Northern Fuerteventura

This 75-mile (120-km) tour offers a rich mix of interesting towns to visit, including Betancuria and Antigua, plus dramatic mountain and coastal scenery. The route starts and finishes at Corralejo. Those starting from southern resorts can join the tour at Antigua and follow it in a clockwise manner leaving extra time to explore Corralejo.

La Casa del Artesano

Leave Corralejo by the road to La Oliva and take the first road right to pass La Casa del Artesano lacemaking centre on reaching the village of Lajares. One member of the family is usually to be found busy making lace and doing embroidery, and the shop here offers a good selection of lace items made on the premises. There is also a coffee shop and restaurant. There are a number of similar centres in this region which is well known for its lacemaking. Notice too the windmills gracing the landscape, which are a feature of this island.

El Cotillo

Continue on to the junction and turn right for El Cotillo. This is a small fishing village with a defensive tower closed to the public. The main interest here lies in the coastline north of the village, seen by taking the *faro* (lighthouse) road. Atlantic rollers surge in and crash into mountains of foam but, surprisingly, there are sheltered lagoons with silver-white sand, which are safe for children. Be aware that nude bathing is commonplace here.

La Oliva

From El Cotillo take the road to La Oliva. Capital of the island for a short period between 1836 and 1860, La Oliva is visited for its church, the Casa de los Coroneles (House of the Colonels) and its modern art museum, the Centro de Arte Canario. Undergoing renovation, the Casa de los Coroneles can be viewed only from a distance. This 18th-century fort-like building, well decked with Canarian balconies, is a 40-room mansion once belonging to the island's military commanders. The Centro de Arte Canario is located in Casa Mane and surrounded by a cactus garden. This well-presented exhibition features modern works by Canarian artists, including César Manrique. *Open daily 1000–1800 (1000–1700 in winter). Closed Sun. Small charge.*

Morro Velosa

Continue south, following signs to Betancuria, enjoying open expansive scenery before reaching the hills. A mountain pass is negotiated just before Betancuria from which there is a diversion up to the Mirador Morro Velosa. This visitor's centre is perched on a mountain peak, affording panoramic views over Fuerteventura's volcanic landscape. Canarian snacks are available from a *tapas* bar and there is a telescope on the terrace. *Open daily 1030–1830 from Dec 2001. Small charge.*

Betancuria

The pass from the mountain descends into Betancuria. Located in a fertile valley, and divided by something quite rare on the island, a stream, Betancuria was the island's first capital under the Spanish until 1834. The island's Norman conqueror, Jean de Béthencourt, founded his capital here at the beginning of the 15th century, away from the coast, to try to escape Berber pirate attacks. But the Berbers were not deterred by the long trek inland and in 1593 sacked the town, destroying the original cathedral, and took 600 captives as slaves. The beautiful present-day church, Iglesia Santa María de Betancuria, is open to visitors daily except Sunday, for 30 minutes every hour – in rotation with the church museum just a short distance away. The church has a beautiful baroque altarpiece and some works of art. Near to the church is the Casa Santa Maria complex, which combines a small museum, a *bodega*, where wine and cheese can be sampled, and craft workshops from 1100–1600. Local produce, such as cactus jam, *mojo* sauces and a variety of fruit liqueurs, can all be purchased here. The old workshops have been converted into a beautiful restaurant (*see page 101*). *Open daily 1000–1800. Small charge.*

Down across the river from the Casa Santa Maria is the archaeological museum, marked by cannons outside. This small museum exhibits remains from the pre-Hispanic culture of the island, including many relics of the Guanches – the original tall, white inhabitants of the islands. Fuerteventura has more Guanche sites and relics than any of the other Canary Islands. *Open Tues–Fri & Sun 0930–1730. Closed Mon and Sat. Small charge.*

The roofless building seen down in the valley left of the road on entering Betancuria is the ruined 15th-century convent of San Buenaventura. It looks much more interesting from the inside with graceful Gothic arches still in place.

Return from Betancuria by the same road over the mountain pass, but this time turn right for Antigua (*see page 106*) at the first junction. From here head north along the road to the capital, Puerto del Rosario. Join the fast ring road around the capital and continue on to Corralejo. This route passes through the extensive sand dunes that lie just south of the resort.

RESTAURANTS

Charly's Fresh Fish £
Very popular. *Calle Cirilo Lopez 3. Tel: 928 541 066. Open Mon–Sat 1200–2230.*

Casa Santa Maria
££ Attractive restaurant serving traditional Canarian food. A little on the expensive side but worth it for a holiday treat. *Casa Santa Maria complex, Betancuria. Tel: 928 878 282. Open daily 1200–1800.*

El Cotillo

Southern Fuerteventura

This 115-mile (185km) car tour takes you along narrow twisting roads, beset by rose-hued rocks and purple-streaked volcanic craters, amongst the crowded hills of the central mountains. On the return journey, Valles de Ortega shows the contrasting face of the island's landscape – soft valleys graced by evergreen palms and fields of exotic fruits.

Jandía is the starting place for this tour, which is easily joined by visitors staying in the south. For those staying in the north, the best option is to use the coastal road down to Puerto del Rosario then head inland to Antigua. The circuit from here, including Tuineje, Pájara and Betancuria, takes in the best of the scenery and many of the places of interest. Return from Betancuria via La Oliva.

CAMEL SAFARI

A popular excursion on Fuerteventura is the camel safari that takes place at La Lajita, which also has an excellent zoo. Treks take place throughout the day according to demand. Camel rides are available for casual callers as well as organised groups. The route sets off beneath an avenue of palms before heading into the open countryside. A buffet lunch is often included with organised tours.

The zoo might seem small but, once inside, the footpath winds and twists through a surprising number of exhibits, which feature monkeys, baboons, flamingos, ostriches, parrots and Nile crocodiles. Feeding the crocodiles takes place around once each week, a little more frequently in summer. Included in the zoo is a tropical plant house with free flying birds as well as a fine cactus garden. Parrot shows take place daily at specified times. Facilities include a snack bar and souvenir shop. *Tel: 928 161 135. Zoo open daily 0900–1930.*

Take the coastal road north soon passing the curious 'gingerbread' house on the right – hardly a César Manrique creation, but probably inspired by him. Once beyond Costa Calma, turn inland following signs to La Pared. Drive now through this terracotta landscape, streaked with shades of olive and a thousand other hues, to reach La Pared (meaning 'the wall'), so-called because in centuries past, the area was divided into two parts, each with its own ruler. A complex was started and then virtually abandoned. Out of curiosity, follow the sign for 'Golf' for a short distance to see the expansive *rambla* in the middle of nowhere.

Pájara

Continue north, enjoying more of the island's unique landscape, to reach Pájara, worth a stop if only for the church and refreshments. If lunch at a fish restaurant is preferred, the fishing village of Puerto de Peña, with a selection of restaurants, is nearby (a 12-mile/20-km diversion).

Rural and tranquil Pájara is not without style. The major attraction is the church, Iglesia de la Virgen de la Regla, the most beautiful on the island. Interior architecture mixes baroque and Gothic but it is the decorative main altar which draws the attention. If it is not illuminated, pop a coin in the meter in the vestibule and see it in all its glory. Motifs decorating the main doorway suggest an Aztec influence. The legend is that Our Lady of Regla comes from Mexico and was donated by a returning emigrant who had amassed a fortune there. *Open daily 0900–1900.*

Outside the church is an old camel-driven *noria* (bucket wheel) for drawing water. Opposite is a delightful stopping place for refreshments. Strolling beyond the church and the car park leads to a pleasant garden with a children's play area. The Centro Cultural of Pájara has a tennis court and swimming and basketball facilities. It also has a bar and restaurant.

Betancuria

Take the road immediately out of Pájara for Betancuria. Prepare for the most scenic road on the island but be warned – this narrow, twisting road hangs from the mountainside on a cornice in parts. It is best to drive with great care. Part-way up is an excellent viewpoint looking down over a disused reservoir in the direction of Puerto de Peña, a good spot to picnic. Save time for Betancuria, the next stop, where there is plenty to see (*page 100*).

Antigua

The onward route slips over a mountain pass where a diversion leads up to Morro Velosa, where a visitor's centre, perched on a mountain peak, affords panoramic views over the nearby countryside (*see page 100*). Head now for Antigua, after which you simply drive down through the palm-dotted valley to Tuineje and back to the coast.

Antigua is a sleepy little town dominated by its church. It comes to life at festival times and particularly throughout May and June when the craftsmen and women meet here to show off their work. The Molino de Antigua cultural centre, lying just to the north of the town, is easily picked out by the large black and white windmill restored to prime condition. The complex encloses a fine cactus garden, a craft shop selling authentic local handicrafts and changing exhibitions of art. There is also a restaurant on site. The windmill is open and can be entered. Some windmills were for drawing water but this type was for making flour by grinding toasted maize to a fine powder, called *gofio* – a staple Canarian food.

WALKING TOURS

A number of walking tours are available to help you explore different aspects of the island. Tours include a hike in a volcanic crater, the desert experience, a dry riverbed walk along a *barranco* (valley), a coast-to-coast walk from Costa Calma and a climb up Witch Mountain at Tindaya. Walkers can only join these trips if they have suitable walking shoes for rough terrain and a bottle for carrying water. *Tel: 298 8868 690. Wed and Fri German only spoken.*

RESTAURANTS

 La Flor de Antigua ££

Recommended locally. Authentic Canarian food. *Calle Obispo 43. Tel: 928 878 168. Open Mon–Sat 1200–2200. Closed on Sundays.*

 El Molino de Antigua ££

Interesting location beside a 200-year-old windmill. Actually a catering school but the general public can try the results in a pleasant rustic setting. *Carretera del Sur (south of Antigua). Tel: 928 878 220.*

Food and drink

Eating out can be relatively cheap, especially in typical Canarian restaurants, though these are thinner on the ground in tourist areas, where international menus predominate. For a real Canarian experience it is better to seek out a restaurant frequented by the locals or head out to inland villages. Local food is delicious and certainly not to be avoided. Many traditional dishes originate from earlier more primitive times when there was a limited variety of ingredients. Later inhabitants introduced new ideas and a wider range of fruit and vegetables, to evolve what has become a very wholesome and delicious cuisine.

LOCAL FOOD

Once a staple food of the pre-Hispanic population, and still a feature in many recipes, is *gofio*, toasted maize or wheat, ground into flour. It was once made into bread, but is now used as a thickener or made into dumplings. Canarian soups are more like stews and are virtually a meal in themselves, so choose carefully if you are aiming for three courses. Fresh vegetables are plentiful as is fish (salt and fresh) which is usually boiled, fried or grilled and served with a *mojo* (pronounced 'moho') sauce. Meats, such as goat, rabbit and pork, are found locally but other meat – steak for example – is imported especially for tourists. Goat's cheese is an important accompaniment to a meal and the Canaries boast many varieties – *queso fresco* (fresh) being a popular choice.

TAPAS

An interesting way to sample a variety of Canarian dishes is to seek out a *tapas* bar – the Spaniards' own version of a fast-food outlet. There are many such bars in local communities, but you will be hard pressed to find one in tourist areas. *Tapas* are served in small portions (*tapa* means 'lid' or small dish) but if something more substantial is required, ask for a medium size – *medio ración* – or a large portion to share between two – a *ración* (pronounced 'rassion'). The problem here is knowing what to ask for, so go armed with the names of some dishes or be brave and choose at random from the display on the counter.

Menu decoder

tapas	snacks
aceitunas en mojo	olives in hot sauce
bocadillo (bocadee-yo)	filled roll
ensalada	salad
helado	ice-cream
perrito caliente	hot-dog

TYPICAL CANARIAN DISHES

cabrito	kid
garbanzas	chickpea stew with meat
potage	thick vegetable soup – may contain added meat
potage de berros	watercress soup
pata de cerdo	roast leg of pork
puchero	meat and vegetable stew
ranchos	noodles, beef and chickpeas
*ropa vieja (*pronounced *'bee-eh-ha')*	chickpeas, vegetables and potatoes (although meat can be added)
caldo de escado	fish, vegetables and maize meal stew
chipirones	small squid
gambas ajillo	garlic prawns
sancocho	salted fish (often cherne, a kind of sea bass) with potatoes and sweet potatoes
conejo al salmorejo	rabbit in hot chilli sauce
lomo	slices of pork
pechuga empanada	chicken breast in crumbs
queso	cheese

DESSERTS

arroz con leche	cold rice pudding
bienmesabe	a mix of honey and almonds (delicious poured over ice-cream)
flan	crème caramel
fruta del tiempo	fresh fruit in season
truchas	turnovers filled with pumpkin jam

Papas arrugadas (small jacket potatoes boiled in very salty water) served with a *mojo picante* (hot chilli sauce) or *mojo verde* (herb and garlic sauce) make an ideal snack at lunch time. Those with a light appetite might find one dish between two is sufficient.

DRINKS

*agua (*pronounced *ah-whah) mineral*	mineral water
con gas/sin gas	fizzy/still
batido	milkshake
café	coffee
con leche	with milk
cortado	small white coffee
descafeinado	decaffeinated
solo	black
cerveza	beer
leche	milk
limonada	lemonade
*naranja (*pronounced *naranha)*	orange juice
ron	local rum
té	tea
vino	wine
tinto	red
rosado	rosé
blanco	white

SPECIALITY DRINKS

bitter kas	similar to Campari but non-alcoholic
guindilla	rum-based cherry liqueur
ronmiel	rum-honey, a local speciality
sangria	can be made with champagne on request
Cocktail Atlantico	rum, dry gin, banana liqueur, blue curaçao, pineapple nectar
Cocktail Canario	rum, banana cream liqueur, orange juice, cointreau, a drop of grenadine
mora	blackberry liqueur

AIRPORT SHOPPING

Fuerteventura: has poor airport shopping facilities. It is better and cheaper to buy all duty-free requirements in shops before you leave.

Lanzarote: has good shopping opportunities in the airport departure lounge but is not especially cheap. This is especially true in the case of wines and spirits, so it is wiser to buy these before departing for the airport.

Shopping

Although part of the EU, both Fuerteventura and Lanzarote, like all the Canary Islands, have a special duty-free status. Accordingly, they are treated as a non-EU region for allowances. Although it is tempting to spend and spend on the duty-free goods that fill the shops, there is a limit to the value of goods (and seperate allowances for tobacco and alcohol) which may be brought back to the UK without attracting tax. These allowances vary, so ask your holiday representative for details of duty-free allowances. If any item exceeds that limit it will be subject to tax on the whole value.

BARGAINING AND COUNTERFEIT GOODS

Expect to bargain in markets and at many of the duty-free shops in tourist resorts. Many prices are highly inflated, often by as much as three or four times, over the manufacturer's recommended price. Beware of counterfeit goods, and treat any bargain-priced electrical goods and cameras as suspect. When spending serious money shop only where a money-back guarantee is on offer, and ensure an international warranty exists and is properly completed.

SOUVENIRS

Those looking for souvenirs which are unique to the island might consider:

- Baskets made from woven banana leaves
- Semiprecious gem stones bought loose or made into jewellery
- Olivina – a local semi-precious stone, available in natural form or as jewellery or ornaments.
- Lace, embroidery or pottery
- Lace and linen table-cloths; freely available on the markets, these are often imported, but they can still be good value.

Kids

Neither island has much to offer children, as far as entertainment specifically geared to their needs is concerned. There are plenty of beaches, though, and stupendous wavy dunes on Fuerteventura. Atlantic rollers may crash on to these shores with mesmerising ferocity and splendour, but there are still havens where children can safely enjoy the delights of splashing around in sheltered water and rock pools. Common to both islands are children's play areas. Most towns and villages, even the smallest, have a modern children's play area somewhere close to the centre. These are often quite innovative in design, well constructed – and buried in sand. They provide an excellent focal point for parents to use, especially when touring by car, and make the often necessary frequent pit stops less fraught.

FUERTEVENTURA

The north and the south of the island are renowned for their extensive sands – plenty of room here for sand castles and beach games. Kite-flying is a favourite occupation in these regions, due to the almost constant breeze. Lots of fun can be gained from the dunes near Corralejo. Sand banks here often rise to heights of 30ft (10m) or more and are superb for sliding and rolling down – but children need strict supervision.

Mini-trains are always an attraction and there are two on the island. One train trundles around Corralejo and out to the dunes, and the other plies between the port at Caleta de Fustes and the inland boundary of the resort.

Children will find plenty of entertainment in a visit to the La Lajita Camel Park and Zoo (*see page 103*).

LANZAROTE

Guinate Tropical Park is the major attraction on the island for children and has more on view than first appears. On display are 1,300 rare and colourful exotic birds, tamarind, monkeys, marmosets and meerkats. Wander the gardens past waterfalls and lagoons then settle down to enjoy the parrot show and maybe some refreshments. *Open daily 1000–1700. Tel: 928 835 500.*

Ride on a camel at Timanfaya National Park (*see page 60*). For a fun time with all the family, swim at Aguapark (*see page 51*), with its pools, chutes and slides. A large car park is available.

A popular children's activity is the Pirate Cruise, operating out of Playa Blanca (*pages 44*). The old wooden galleon, the *Marea Errota*, is the base for games, dressing up as pirates, and enjoying a hearty lunch.

TIP! There is a go-kart track just off the road from Arrecife to San Bartolomé. A free bus is available, picking up at various points in Puerto del Carmen and Costa Teguise. *Tel: 928 520 022.* Also Gran Karting Club between Tias and Puerto del Carmen. *Snack bar. Tel: 619 759 946. Open daily 1100–2200.* Be sure to check that your insurance covers this sport.

Sports and activities

CYCLING

Cycles can be hired at most resorts. Both islands provide opportunities for easy cycling as well as more challenging routes through the hills.

FISHING

Big-game fishing is available from most of the major ports, including Corralejo, on Fuerteventura, and Playa Blanca, Puerto del Carmen and Puerto Calero on Lanzarote.

GOLF

There is just one 18-hole course on Lanzarote, outside Costa Teguise: *Club de Golf, Carretera Costa Teguise–Tahice, Costa Teguise. Tel: 928 590 512.*

HORSE RIDING

Lanzarote has two riding schools (*see page 32*).

SCUBA DIVING

- Lanzarote: Calypso Diving, Costa Teguise, arranges free pool sessions and excursions from all resorts.
- Fuerteventura: facilities in Corralejo, at the main port, and in Jandía.

SURFING AND WINDSURFING

The coastline of Famara, in the north west of Lanzarote, offers some of the island's best conditions for surfing. **Surf School Lanzarote** offers a day's excursion, with tuition, wetsuit and board hire and picnic lunch for all ages. Whether you're 7 or 77, the professional instructors of Surf School can have you riding the waves with the best of them. Ask your holiday representative for further details.

Windsurfing facilities are available in most resorts – as a rule, the south-easterly-facing resorts have the quieter conditions preferred by beginners.

WALKING

Two walking trails have been established within the Timanfaya National Park. These are guided walks undertaken at regular times but booking is essential. Both walks are free of charge and commentary is in Spanish and English.

Tremesan Trail: this 2-mile (3-km) trail takes around 2 hours and explores the area of the park near to where the camel rides take place. Commentary along the way relates to the extent of the lava flows, the alignment of volcanoes and the slow process of the establishment of vegetation. Tour days: Monday, Wednesday and Friday starting at 1000 from the Visitor's Centre near Mancha Blanca. *Tel: 928 840 839 (office manned Mon–Sun 0900–1900).*

Ruta del Litoral: a longer trail at 5.6 miles (9km), requiring about 5 hours. This starts at Playa del Paso and follows along the coast to explore the littoral zone. Good footwear, water and light food is required to undertake this walk. The walk can only be arranged by calling personally at the Visitor's Centre (*see page 73*).

Festivals and events

There is nothing the Canarians enjoy more than a good fiesta. Any event of significance is celebrated and turned into a street party. Some fiestas have deep religious significance but most are a lively mixture of fun and exuberance.

Every village celebrates the feast day of its own patron saint, and there are local and national days to celebrate too. Carnaval (Carnival) is the greatest and most colourful of them all. It takes place in February or March, to coincide with the start of Lent, and celebrations take place across the island, culminating in a grand fancy-dress party and masked parade, which goes on for hours.

Carnival is a celebration for the people by the people. The brightest and best of the Carnival parades take place in the capital cities, in Puerto del Rosario on Fuerteventura and in Arrecife on Lanzarote. Parades are held too in just about all the major towns.

Other important celebrations include:

- Ironman: A triathlon, the second toughest in the world, which takes place towards the end of May. Competitors from countries far and near participate. It is organised by La Santa, a well-known Danish sports centre used by professional sportspeople in training.

- Canaries Day, 30 May: There are sports competitions, concerts, dances in typical costume, games and festival food.

- Festival of Dolores: On a par with carnival in terms of scale, this celebration begins on 15 September for the duration of the week. Thousands are dressed in local costume and walk from their villages to Mancha Blanca, singing and dancing on the way. There is a craft fair, concerts and fun stalls.

 Ask at the Tourist Office for a list of festivals. There is almost certainly one taking place somewhere on the island during your stay.

CANARY WRESTLING

This unusual sport is very popular on Lanzarote, with many clubs holding competitions. Traditionally, the wrestling – a cross between sumo and ordinary wrestling – takes place in a sand-covered arena and involves a team of 12. The loser is the one who touches the ground with any part of the body (apart from their feet) during a hold.

CONCERTS ON LANZAROTE

There is a full programme of concerts and cultural events held in the auditorium of Jameos del Agua. *For details contact Insular Cabildo Centro de Cultura, Arrecife. Tel: 928 804 095.*

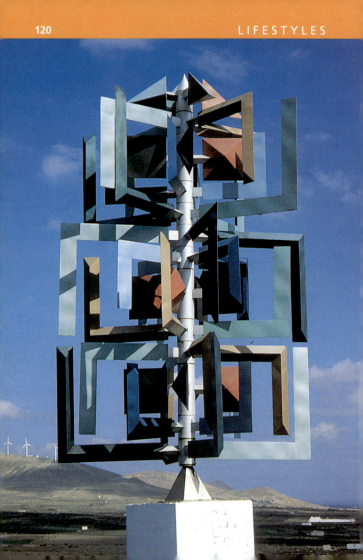

Taking better holiday photos

All professional photographers know that it's not the camera that takes good pictures, it's the photographer. David Bailey takes stunning pictures using a cheap throwaway camera, and we all know the show-offs with the expensive lenses who still cannot take a decent picture. The truth is that camera technology is now so good that anyone can take top-quality pictures, if you follow a few simple rules.

Choose the correct film for the lighting conditions: film stock is available in different speeds depending on the lighting conditions. Fast film – 100 ASA – is best for the bright light you will experience at most resorts, where the brightness of the sun is enhanced by reflections from the sand and water. Slow film – 400 ASA – is better for indoor photography or anywhere that you would need to use flash – for architectural shots in shade, for example. If, like most photographers, you want to take a mix of indoor and outdoor pictures, buy an intermediate speed of film – 200 ASA is ideal.

Use light to your advantage: everybody knows the golden rule that you should never take a picture directly into the sun – ideally the sun should be behind you, so that the light falls where you want it – on the subject of your photograph. But all rules can be broken to advantage: shooting into the sun can be used to create a back-lit effect, whereby the sun creates a silhouette around the subject – even more effective at sunset.

Use shadows: the opposite of sunlight is shadow, and many professional photographers prefer to take pictures early in the day, when the sun is low and the shadows are deep, rather than during the main part of the day, when every detail is equally lit. Shadows enhance the details of sculpture and architecture: even a boring wall can become an interesting subject if shadows enhance the texture.

Avoid the harsh light of the hottest part of the day: another reason for avoiding harsh sunlight is that it has the effect of bleaching colour; that is why the blue sky looks white on your photographs, and why intensely coloured flowers look pale and washed out. The best time for photography is early in the morning and later in the afternoon, in the soft magical hours before dusk. If you do take photos during the day, wait for the sun to go behind a cloud, which helps to diffuse and soften the harsh light.

Get up close to your subject: the big mistake that every amateur photographer makes is to try and cram too much into the picture. Good photographs are ones that choose a detail that stands for the whole. Take a picture of a stone sculpture, rather than the whole of the church façade; of a single orchid rather than the whole of the flower-filled meadow; of a water-filled rockpool rather than the whole sweep of beach.

Catch the family unawares: try to avoid the obvious pose when taking pictures of your friends and family. Better still, try to avoid posing them at all – candid photographs (those that are taken without the subject being aware) are often far better than posed ones, because the subject is relaxed and looks more like their normal selves, rather than wearing an artificial smile or a cheesy grin. Take pictures of your family as they eat, shop and fool around – bringing life and movement into the photograph.

Tell a story: ask yourself, as you compose the picture, what is this picture about and will it interest another person? Think like a photo journalist as you look for picture subjects that will arouse curiosity and make the viewer want to take a second look. You want people to say, as they look at your pictures, 'that is interesting', not 'what a bore!'.

And finally … use a reputable film-processing company. Don't trust your precious holiday pictures to any old express film-processing service, or the investment you have made in good-quality film stock and careful composition will be thrown away. If in doubt, wait until you get home before having your pictures developed, and use a processor whose standards you know and trust.

Getting there

The cheapest way to get to Lanzarote or Fuerteventura is to book a package holiday with one of the leading tour operators, such as Thomas Cook or JMC. Tour operators specialising in the Canary Islands offer flight only deals or combined flight-and-accommodation packages at prices that are hard to beat by booking direct. If your travelling times are flexible, and if you can avoid the school holidays, you can also find some very cheap last-minute deals using websites such as www.thomascook.com.

BY AIR

The Canary Islands are a 4-hour flight from the UK. The majority of visitors to the islands use charter companies, which operate from nearly all of the UK's regional airports. Only the Spanish national carrier, Iberia Airlines, offers scheduled flights to the Canaries, though this usually means changing in Madrid or Barcelona. Iberia's UK office is at Venture House, 27–29 Glasshouse Street, London W1R 6JU, tel: 020 7830 0011; fax: 020 7413 1261.

BY SHIP

Trasmediterranea runs once a week from Cadiz to Gran Canaria, Lanzarote and Tenerife. Trasmediterranea's UK agent is Southern Ferries, First Floor, 179 Piccadilly, London W1V 9DB, tel: 020 7491 4968; fax 020 7491 3502. Early bookings are necessary for school holidays and at Carnival time (February). Tickets include all meals during the voyage.

INTER ISLAND SERVICES

A complex network of inter-island ferries and hydrofoils links the seven main islands of the Canaries, and schedules change very regularly, so you need to check times locally. Most of the inter-islands services are operated by Trasmediterranea (website: www.trasmediterranea.es) or the Fred Olsen Line (timetable details and on-line booking on the companies website: www.fredolsen.es). The local airline Binter Canarias provides regular flights between the islands (Aeropuerto de Gran Canaria, Parcela 9 del ZIMA, Apartado 50, 35230 Gran Canaria, tel: 928 57960, fax: 928 579603, website: www.bintercanarias.es).

First-time traveller's guide

BEFORE YOU GO

Holidays should be about fun and relaxation, so avoid last-minute panics and stress by making your preparations well in advance.

Passports: Make sure that your passports are up to date and have at least three months left to run (to be safe, six months is even better). All children (new-born babies upwards) need their own passport now, unless they are already included on the passport of the person they are travelling with – in which case they can continue to travel abroad with the passport holder until they reach the age of 16. Remember that it takes at least three weeks to renew or obtain a passport. Ring the Passport Agency on 0990 210410, or access its website (www.ukpa.gov.uk), for details of the current passport processing times, and how to apply for a passport or renew an existing one.

Money: You will need some currency before you go, especially if your flight gets you to your destination at the weekend or late in the day after the banks have closed. Traveller's cheques are the safest way to carry money because the money will be refunded if the cheques are lost or stolen. To buy traveller's cheques or exchange money at a bank you may need to give up to a week's notice, depending on the quantity of foreign currency you require. You can exchange money at the airport before you depart. You should also make sure that your credit, charge and debit cards are up to date – you do not want them to expire mid holiday – and that your credit limit is sufficient to allow you to make those holiday purchases. Don't forget, too, to check your PIN numbers in case you haven't used them for a while – you may want to draw money from cash dispensers while you are away. Ring your bank or card company and they will help you out.

INSURANCE

Have you got sufficient cover for your holiday? Check that your policy covers you adequately for loss of possessions and valuables, for activities you might want to try – such as scuba-diving, horse-riding, or watersports – and for emergency medical and dental treatment, including flights home if required.

HEALTH MATTERS

You do not need inoculations to travel within Europe, but it is worth checking that you and your family are up to date with the basics, such as tetanus. If you take prescription medicines, make sure you have enough to last the whole trip. Consider packing a small first-aid kit containing plasters, antiseptic cream, travel sickness pills, insect repellent and/or bite-relief cream, upset stomach remedies, painkillers and sun lotions.

PETS

Remember to make arrangements for the care of your pets while you are away – book them into a reputable cat or dog hotel, or make arrangements with a trustworthy neighbour to ensure that they are properly fed, watered and exercised while you are on holiday.

SECURITY

Take sensible precautions to prevent your house being burgled while you are away:

- Cancel milk, newspapers and other regular deliveries so that post and milk does not pile up on the doorstep, indicating that you are away.
- Let the postman know where to leave parcels and bulky mail that will not go through your letterbox – ideally with a next-door neighbour.
- If possible, arrange for a friend or neighbour to visit regularly, closing and opening curtains in the evening and morning, and switching lights on and off to give the impression that the house is being lived in.
- Consider buying electrical timing devices that will switch lights and radios on and off, again to give the impression that there is someone in the house.
- Let Neighbourhood Watch representatives and the police know that you will be away so that they can keep an eye on your home.
- If you have a burglar alarm, make sure that it is serviced and working properly and is switched on when you leave (you may find that your insurance policy requires this). Ensure that a neighbour is able to gain access to the alarm to turn it off if it is set off accidentally.
- If you are leaving cars unattended, put them in a garage, if possible, and leave a key with a neighbour in case the alarm goes off.

AIRPORT PARKING AND ACCOMMODATION

If you intend to leave your car in an airport car park while you are away, or stay the night at an airport hotel before or after your flight, you should book well ahead to take advantage of discounts or cheap off-airport parking. Airport accommodation gets booked up several weeks in advance, especially during the height of the holiday season. Check whether the hotel offers free parking for the duration of the holiday – often the savings made on parking costs can significantly reduce the accommodation price.

PACKING TIPS

Baggage allowances vary according to the airline, destination and the class of travel, but 20 kilos per person is the norm for luggage that is carried in the hold (it usually tells you what the weight limit is on your ticket). You are also allowed one item of cabin baggage weighing no more than 5 kilos, and measuring 46 by 30 by 23 cm (18 by 12 by 9 inches). In addition, you can usually carry your duty-free purchases, umbrella, handbag, coat, camera, etc, as hand baggage. Large items – surfboards, golf-clubs, collapsible wheelchairs and pushchairs – are usually charged as extras and it is a good idea to let the airline know in advance that you want to bring these.

CHECK-IN, PASSPORT CONTROL AND CUSTOMS

First-time travellers can often find airport security intimidating, but it is all very easy really.

- Check-in desks usually open two or three hours before the flight is due to depart. Arrive early for the best choice of seats.

- Look for your flight number on the TV monitors in the check-in area, and find the relevant check-in desk. Your tickets will be checked and your luggage taken. Take your boarding card and go to the departure gate. Here your hand luggage will be X-rayed and your passport checked.

- In the departure area, you can shop and relax, but watch the monitors that tell you when to board – usually about 30 minutes before take-off. Go to the departure gate shown on the monitor and follow the instructions given to you by the airline staff.

Editorial and production

Project Management: Dial House Publishing
Managing Editor for Thomas Cook Publishing: Deborah Parker
Design: Wenham Arts
Editing and proofreading: Dial House Publishing
Picture research: Michelle Warrington
Map Editor for Thomas Cook Publishing: Bernard Horton
Maps redrawn by Polly Senior Cartography

2002 Edition

Project Management: Cambridge Publishing Management Ltd
Layout and repro: Cambridge Publishing Management Ltd
Printed and bound by: Artes Gráficas Elkar, Loiu, Spain

Acknowledgements

We would like to thank all the photographers, picture libraries and organisations
for the loan of the photographs reproduced in this book, to whom copyright in
the photograph belongs:

B and E Anderson (pages 3, 9, 16, 20, 27, 28, 32, 36, 40, 43, 44, 47, 49, 55,
    59, 61, 64, 67, 70, 74, 76, 83, 91, 92, 101, 102, 106, 107, 112, 115, 117,
    120 and 123);

JMC (pages 6, 18, 50, 80, 88 and 108);

Paul Murphy (pages 25, 34 and 105);

Adele Evans (pages 39 and 69);

J Allan Cash (pages 62, 79, 87 and 118);

Eric Roberts (pages 85 and 95).